'FRB'
A
Portrait of
Bishop Russell Barry

by

Frank H. West

Archdeacon of Newark 1947-62
Bishop of Taunton 1962-1977

GROVE BOOKS

BRAMCOTE   NOTTS.

CONTENTS

PHOTOS

Facing page 52: 'FRB', Army Chaplain 1919
Facing page 53: 'FRB', Canon of Westminster 1937
Facing page 68: 'FRB', Bishop of Southwell 1951
Facing page 69: 'FRB', with the Archbishop of Grodno, 1947
and
'FRB', saying his office a month before his death 1976
(Photo supplied by Mr. Russell Kelly, 'FRB''s grandson)

First Impression March 1980

ISBN 0 905422 74 0

DEDICATION

To my wife

whose marriage to me 'FRB' solemnized over thirty years ago,

and to my children,

Frances Mary and Roger, whom he baptized.

ACKNOWLEDGMENTS

I am greatly indebted to a host of the friends, acquaintances and former colleagues of Bishop F. R. Barry who responded to my invitation in the Press to send me their reminiscences and impressions of the Bishop. I am grateful to Canon F. W. Dillistone, Canon Douglas Vicary, the Bishop of Bath and Wells, and to my wife, for reading through the original typescript and providing me with much-needed criticism and advice on the text and my general handling of the subject. Mr. W. R. G. Pullen, the Registrar of Westminster Abbey, kindly allowed me to read through the Chapter Minutes covering the period when Canon Barry was a member of the Chapter and Canon Alan Wilkinson generously sent me all the references to F. R. Barry which he had gathered together when writing his invaluable book, *The Church of England in the First World War*. This portrait of Russell Barry would not yet have seen the light of day were it not for the untiring efforts and professional expertise of Mrs. Valerie Watson who, on top of many other commitments, typed and retyped successive texts with unfailing patience. My wife, fortunately and predictably, regarded it as a privilege to entertain Bishop Barry as an ever-present, if invisible, guest in our home, for that is what he has been, since my retirement as Bishop of Taunton two years ago. So much has he been with us that many of his well-remembered quips and mannerisms have become embedded in our domestic parlance!

Frank West
Aldbourne]
November 1979

3

INTRODUCTION

I was one of Bishop Barry's archdeacons from 1947 to 1962. Previously I had only met him once. That was in 1935 when he offered me the curacy of St. John's, Smith Square—an offer which I refused with all the conceit of youth, because I was told that on Sunday mornings the church would be full when it had been advertised in the Press that the Rector was preaching, and nearly empty when it was the turn of the curate. So I missed the opportunity of getting to know him in his pre-Southwell days; but that tour round his parish in his company was an unforgettable experience. I had, of course, been an enthusiastic reader of his books since my student days.

It is said that a master is never a hero to his valet. By the same token a bishop is unlikely to be a saint to his archdeacon. Certainly in the fifteen years I was with Bishop Barry I had plenty of opportunity of observing his weaknesses, and he had weaknesses both as a man and as a bishop. Although this memoir is far from being a hagiography, I can truthfully say that I regard it as one of the great privileges of my life that I was so closely associated with him for so long a period. He has been the most powerful influence on my way of thinking ever since. No one who has read, marked, learned, and inwardly digested, what Russell Barry wrote and said over a period of sixty years can be taken by surprise by any circumstances in which he may find himself here on earth. Russell's faith was all the more stimulating and strengthening because, like Cranmer thrusting his hand into the flames before he was tied to the stake, he had gone out of his way to test his own in adversity.

When a distinguished man writes his autobiography in the last decade of his life, he may discourage other people undertaking a biography for some time after his death. How true this is of Hensley Henson! When Barry at the instigation of some of his friends, of whom I was one, wrote *Period of my Life* in 1970, we took it for granted that he had forfeited any chance of finding a biographer in the near future, though most of us did not feel he had done himself justice nor sufficiently disclosed himself in his autobiography. So when the invitation came to me from the Chapter of Southwell Minster to undertake a memoir, I was not only surprised but embarrassed. However, after reading *Period of my Life* once again, glancing through the many tributes, anecdotes and impressions which flowed in after I had announced my intentions, I came to realize that I had been set a worthwhile even though daunting task.

To begin with, although Barry had revealed more of himself in his autobiography than at any time before, his natural modesty and reserve had restrained him from telling all. As was to be expected, *Period of my Life* revealed much more of what Russell thought about the world than what the world thought about him. Although he was not unaware of his frailties, he was much less aware of the wealth of affection which he had aroused in other people throughout his life. The classic example of understatement in his book was when he wrote off his reputation for gallantry on the Somme with the five words, 'They thought I was brave'.[1] Russell could hardly tell his readers in his own book that when he was 'fobbed off' with the D.S.O. in 1916 there was a near mutiny amongst the Manchesters whom he had served as a padre. But that is how a major who later became a clergyman described the reaction of the regiment when it came through that their chaplain was not to receive the highest award for valour after all.

I have had to contend with a number of other difficulties as well, chief of which is that Barry, living as he did to the age of eighty-five, outlived most of his contemporaries. The number of people who can remember him in his army days are very few indeed and even his Knutsford students are most of them octogenarians. He was the eldest child of a first marriage. His siblings are all dead and he was a big boy when his two half-brothers were born. So it is that I have very few sources of information about his childhood to tap. What did the other boys at Bradfield think of him? No one will ever know, although I seem to remember that Eric Hamilton, once Dean of Windsor, a school contemporary, thought he was then a 'funny little thing'. This seems to me to be a typical verdict on a small boy who wasn't good at games by an older boy who was.

All Russell's early papers, sermons, notes and photographs were destroyed in the blitz. Few of his letters from any period of his life have survived, perhaps fortunately for his biographer because his handwriting was almost illegible. G. M. Trevelyan once said that he had put all that he had got into his books and had not taken much trouble with letters to his friends. The same is probably true of Barry. He never kept a diary.

On one point I had to wrestle with myself. Ought I to commit to print a selection of the host of stories told about him in the diocese, many of which originated from impromptu answers given to questions he could not hear on account of his deafness? This deafness was certainly a major tragedy in his life and was largely responsible for his not being translated to a more venerable diocese. In the end I decided to include a selection at the risk of being accused of bad taste, not only because they are funny but because any picture of F. R. Barry as a man and as a bishop would be lacking without them. They, as much as anything else, account for the affection in which he was held in the diocese and have helped to embellish the legend which has grown up around him.

For half a century, Russell Barry was a champion of the liberal tradition in the Church of England, an ingredient which has survived waves of evangelical enthusiasm and anglo-catholic authoritarianism since the time of Hooker, and without which the Church of England, as it has been known for four centuries, would cease to exist, and certainly would not make its distinctive contribution to Catholic Christendom. That liberal tradition seems to be out of favour today. Adverse conditions are putting the Church on the defensive. It is for this very reason that the life and work of F. R. Barry should not be allowed to slip into oblivion in this last quarter of the twentieth century.

Frank West

[1] *Period of my Life*, p.54.

1. EARLY LIFE

I

On All Saints' Day 1941 Frank Russell Barry was enthroned Bishop of Southwell in his Cathedral. As the procession singing 'Through the Night of Doubt and Sorrow' wended its way round the great Norman church, it passed close to the tomb of Archbishop Sandys who had died in the neighbouring manor house when the Spanish Armada was sailing up the Channel. In the weeks that lay ahead the new bishop was to console himself with his reflections on that tomb. He had come to the diocese of Southwell in the darkest days of the conflict. The Germans were launching an offensive on Moscow with the intention of driving the Russians out of the war before Christmas. Shipping losses in the Atlantic had reached an unprecedented level. Pearl Harbour was two months ahead and the Americans had not yet entered the war on Britain's side.

Members of the large congregation who, despite petrol rationing and other wartime restrictions, had come to welcome their new bishop must have been wondering what sort of man had been sent to them. One glance at his slight figure convinced them that there was little outward resemblance between him and his predecessor. Dr. Mosley in deportment and style looked every inch a bishop. In cope and mitre he seemed to the manner born. Courtly in appearance, when he and his wife greeted guests on formal occasions, he was gracious and easy with people of all sorts. Russell Barry, who could not bring himself to wear a mitre at his enthronement, gave the impression that the sooner he discarded episcopal attire the better he would be pleased, and that if an eye were not kept on him he would slip out of a solemn procession to some hidey-hole in a corner of the church.[1]

Dr. Mosley had come to the episcopate by way of a succession of great urban parishes. Bishop Barry's previous parochial experience had been in churches which not many of his clergy would have described as ordinary. The *Nottingham Guardian* referred to his fame as preacher and writer. It did not add that his preaching had been confined mainly to eclectic rather than to parochial congregations. His books had made a great stir in the years after the First War and he was acclaimed one of the most influential prophets of the 1920s and 30s. But his writings had appealed more to liberal churchmen than to anglo-catholics and evangelicals. Liberal bishops have always been suspect to the rank and file of their clergy who, for some strange reason, are inclined to rate scholarship in a bishop rather low in their list of priorities. Without doubt the new bishop would be in the liberal tradition.

II

Bishop Barry's enthronement sermon made a good impression on the congregation. The *Nottingham Guardian* remarked on his deep resonant voice curiously at variance with his slight physique. On the following

---

1 This in fact did happen on one occasion in Newark Parish Church when the church-wardens, under the impression they were leading the bishop to his throne in the sanctuary, turned inwards at the altar rails and bowed low, only to find to their bewilderment that he had completely disappeared. He had slipped into a return stall at the entrance to the choir.

Monday morning a wider public learnt that the new bishop had urged a more militant policy on the Church. 'A church content to be on the defensive,' he said in the course of his sermon, 'has committed suicide . . . the methods of our church have been primarily pastoral. They must now be primarily evangelistic.' Clearly the Lord had raised up a prophet in the land through which the middle reaches of the River Trent flowed. But what sort of a man lay behind this reputation for preaching and writing?

The fifth Bishop of Southwell was indeed a complex character, as his diocese was soon to discover. For this his childhood experiences were at least partly responsible. On his own admission the death of his mother when he was eight years of age left a permanent scar upon him. 'I now scarcely remember my mother,' he wrote seventy years later, 'for she died in 1898 at the birth of my youngest brother, Gerald, having borne six children in eight years (the Church then, and that generation, believed that what we now accept as a Christian duty [i.e. family planning] was contrary to the law of God . . .) My mother's death was a shattering blow to the young family and most of all to our father, left desolate with five small children on his hands . . . for me it was a deeply traumatic experience, leaving me an unhappy and introverted child who could not easily relate to other children, making me hate school instead of enjoying it. I think I have never really recovered from being left in childhood without a mother.'[1] This is undoubtedly true. In spite of his triumphant record during the first World War, his popularity with soldiers and students and his rapid promotion in war and peace, Russell, partly because of his increasing deafness and partly because he found so many of his episcopal duties irksome, affected the manner of an unhappy child at a party and a rather waiflike demeanour.

The death of his mother, dramatized by the father in true Victorian fashion, was not the only traumatic experience in Russell's childhood. For several years after his bereavement Duncan Barry came to lean heavily on the company of his bright little boy. Then, very properly, he married again and the children of his first marriage deeply resented the intrusion of a stepmother, hard as she tried to gain their confidence. This in the end she succeeded in doing. But many years later Russell told his wife that for months on end at home and at school he had wept himself to sleep. To the end of his life he seemed to be inviting sympathy; 'the wretched Bishop' was an epithet which he most frequently applied to himself. Although he was able to climb to the top of Great Gable until well into his seventies, he sometimes used to grope and stagger back to the sanctuary after preaching as if he found difficulty in making the journey through the choir stalls. Yet when sympathy was offered, as it often was by solicitous wives, he seemed reluctant to accept it.

Victorian family life with its possessiveness, its sentimentality, and its absence of psychological understanding, is difficult now to assess. Duncan Barry never forgave his son Gerald for the death of his wife; and Gerald himself, according to Russell, carried a guilty conscience with him all through his life once he discovered that his mother had died in giving him

1 *Period of my Life,* p.22.

birth. It never seemed to occur to the father that he, rather than the infant, had been responsible for the pregnancy which ended in the death of his wife.

Russell had been brought up in country rectories and at heart he remained a countryman all his days, but, like Cyril Garbett and Geoffrey Fisher, his affection for the village was largely nostalgic. The smell of a harvest festival evoked affectionate memories and he missed the odour of the oil lamp in the electrified village churches of his diocese. But, although he was to enjoy visiting country churches, and, with his father's example always in the back of his mind, became the champion of the rural ministry in the councils of the Church, he was never quite at home in their pulpits. Unlike St. Mary's, Oxford, and St. John's, Smith Square, they did not provide him with the kind of audience that brought the best out of him. 'I've just been preaching to two old women and a batty girl' he once moaned with typical Barryan pungency and exaggeration after keeping an engagement in a country church.

Russell has left behind him few recollections of his schooldays at Bradfield. Distinction in athletics, that passport to public school popularity, eluded him. He reached the sixth form in his second year, eventually became a prefect and acted in the Greek play for which the school is famous. But he must have found the lack of privacy irksome. Quoting Gibbon, he described the public school of his day as 'the triumph of barbarism and religion.' He *was* religious, but there was not a trace of barbarism in his make-up. Such boys as he suffered from the rough-and-tumble of public school life.

In the Berkshire woodlands which surrounded the school, Russell discovered a refuge from the hubbub of the boys' common room in which he could pursue his own thoughts undisturbed. 'It would have been hard,' he wrote, 'to grow up in those surroundings without being permeated with a "sense of something far more deeply interfused"—the bluebell woods in May can be a theophany. It gave me a heightened sensitivity to and reverence towards natural beauty and that is surely a gateway to faith and worship.'[1] By the end of his schooldays Russell had become a disciple of Wordsworth and it gave him great pleasure fifty years later to be asked to give the address at the Wordsworth Centenary service.

In 1915 he wrote back from the desert to the dons of Oriel:

'The spaciousness and loneliness is wonderful. It carries one right out of our crowded lives and opens to us doors in heaven. There is a marvellous majesty of silence and eternity within the temporal order, a mysteriousness which is vocal. It is sphinx-like and irresistable. I always supposed that there would be an intolerable monotony of yellow. Instead it is incredibly coloured, pink and purple and pale green. Somehow it is always asking questions, especially at night and early morning . . . the dew is always very heavy and the sun breaks suddenly over it about 6.30 turning to blue and gold all that he touches, and he flames out equally suddenly in the early evening and darkness

[1] *Period of my Life*, p.37.

comes without any twilight. Then the stars come out and to me the stars are the greatest of discoveries . . . the stars are pitiless and must be placated. They are masters of magical spells and rain down influences. One begins to understand the astral religions and their development in the mysticism of Posidonius.'

In the hedgerows of East Anglia and even more in the woods around Bradfield he had flirted with pantheism. In the wide open spaces of the desert he came to realize why the prophets of Israel and Islam were monotheists. His theology was always derivative.

III

Russell went up to Oxford in the autumn of 1908 with a major scholarship at Oriel. Oriel, in spite of its association with the fathers of the Oxford Movement, was not regarded as one of the leading colleges in the University. It was small in numbers, modest and friendly, drawing its students from the less distinguished public schools and from homes which, though cultured, were certainly not wealthy. But in the year Russell went up there were three other freshmen who were to achieve Firsts in Greats four years later. It was the kind of friendly college in which societies proliferate and one in which a shy boy, rather young for his age, would immediately feel at home.

At Oriel, Russell found himself. These, to use his own expression, were the golden days of the University. Perhaps the undergraduates were not as carefree and insulated from the outside world as they are now sometimes thought to have been. Judging by the motions in the Oriel debating societies, like those of the Union at that time, they were not unaware of the frictions, political, economic, and social, which distracted the country in the last years before the war. The College Mission in the East End gave them a nodding acquaintance with their contemporaries in the slums of London. They debated a motion that the working classes should be admitted to the University, apparently in ignorance of the fact that there was no law prohibiting members of the lower orders from matriculating if they could. It was the means to shoulder the expense of a university education which kept them away. In another debate, it was moved 'that this house would welcome the retirement from politics of the Rt. Hon. David Lloyd George'.[1] From what Russell was to write in a pamphlet on war aims four years later, it is quite clear that he had been keeping abreast of the great political issues of the day: the constitutional crisis of 1911, the growing menace of German militarism, industrial unrest, and the threat of civil war in Ireland.

But radical as he was becoming in politics and religion and naturally critical of any institution in which he was concerned, it is quite clear that he found the Oxford of his undergraduate days entirely congenial, along with most of his contemporaries taking his privileged status there very much for granted. Some of his best after-dinner speeches at the annual dinner of

1 Throughout Russell's time at Oriel, Lloyd George was the most controversial political figure in the constitutional crisis which raged during the last months of the life of Edward VII and into the reign of George V.

the Oxford Society in Nottingham forty years later were wistfully nostalgic. He spoke with evident appreciation of 'the cheerful chap about the quad' who was not much else.[1]

Russell joined all the college societies and became president of several of them. He wrote learned papers and took an active part in the debates. He was a frequent and popular speaker, though strangely he never seems to have tried his hand at the Union. On the motion that, 'This house has its doubts' Mr. Barry was 'in his happiest vein and had the large house convulsed in a very short time.' What exactly his doubts were in 1910 we shall never know. But it can be taken for granted that the youthful speaker who, many years later, as a bishop, was to tell an ordination candidate who boasted he had never had a doubt in his life, that he should go away and collect a few, took a very different line from the Reverend Ronald Knox, Chaplain of Trinity College, who opposed the motion. A few years later Knox shelved his own doubts by surrendering to the Church of Rome. On this occasion his speech was described in the college journal as 'brilliant and whimsical'. The diverging paths which these two clever young Christians were to take in later life is foreshadowed by the different parts they played in that college debate in 1910.

At the Arnold Society, Russell gave a lecture on sacerdotalism which, along with clericalism, he was later to regard as the curse of the Church throughout its history. Whether or not he had reached this conclusion in his undergraduate days we are not to know. To the surprise of those who only knew him as a liberal and very unconventional bishop, he confessed in his autobiography that at Oxford,

> 'I passed through a silly phase of ecclesiastical spikery, attending the more extreme Oxford churches and morbidly interested in ceremonial. It was something that had to be worked out of the system, and I very quickly got over it. Some men, unhappily, never do get over it, and go through life as religious adolescents.'[2]

In his third year as president of the Arnold Society, he noted with approval in the college magazine the willingness of some of the freshmen 'to give of their valuable talent instead of hiding it under the bushel of timidity.' In the discussions which followed the lectures the third year undergraduate had already adopted the encouraging elder brother attitude towards students junior to himself which was to characterize his relationship with ex-service candidates for ordination at Knutsford ten years later.

In spite of the catholicity of his tastes and interests—he read a paper on Botticelli to the Chameleon Society 'with great eloquence and fluency'—and his full participation in the life of the college, he gained his First in Greats in 1912. Three others in the college were placed in this class and it was noted in the Oriel *Record* that this was the strongest year since 1903. As by this time his thoughts were moving in the direction of ordination, he

---

[1] Twelve years later, after the War, undergraduates ranged themselves light-heartedly on the side of privilege and establishment by manning buses, trams, and trains, during the General Strike. This in itself reveals the wide gap between the mentality of the undergraduate of the first quarter of this century and that of today.

[2] *Period of my Life,* p.44

stayed up an extra year to read Theology. In the summer of 1913, the Editor of the *Record* writes,

> 'We have much pleasure in welcoming our new fellow, Mr. F. R. Barry, formerly a scholar of this College. Mr. Barry served the College well during his undergraduate days, having been president of the Arnold Society, the Plantagenet Society and the Butler Society and a member of the committee of the Amalgamated Clubs. We congratulate the College on the accession of strength which Mr. Barry's appointment will bring it. We wish him many years of useful service as a "Don".'

Perhaps in those inverted commas there is a suggestion that the new fellow, still so youthful and debonair in appearance and manner, was likely to make a very un-donnish don.

IV

There is today a difference of opinion about the value of the educational system of which Russell had taken full advantage when he graduated in 1912. The assumption that it was the best possible education ever devised by civilized man has recently been challenged by Correlli Barnett, amongst others, on the grounds that the obsession with the classics in nineteenth century public schools and universities is one of the contributory causes of the decline in British power since 1870. Gathorne Hardy in his *Public School Phenomenon* thought otherwise. 'Classical education,' he wrote, 'provides not just the richness of a great literature and study of a long and varied history and, once Greek is included, mathematics, philosophy and drama, but also logic, discrimination, love of language and its precise, witty and sensible use and interpretation, a whole range of intellectual disciplines and qualities, ways of thinking which go beyond all subjects and can be brought to bear on any of them.' Russell himself would have subscribed to this view and anyone who heard him speak to an intelligent audience or read any of his books would realize that, both in the spoken and written word, he was an exemplary exponent of the classical tradition. In his autobiography, Russell quotes Sir David Rose, his tutor in Philosophy, as saying to him after he had got his First in Greats, 'You will soon forget all you have learnt, but there is one thing that Greats will have done for you. You will always know when a man is talking nonsense.' Commenting on Sir David's prognostication, Russell was to write rather grimly, 'We have not lacked opportunities for testing that.'[1]

Russell read quickly and remembered what he had read, thereby demonstrating the falsity of his tutor's prediction. The pages of his books were heavily underlined and notes were scribbled in the margins in his illegible hand and all over the title pages. But there was one range of subjects which always remained beyond his understanding, and that was everything covered by the word 'technology'. He was completely devoid of any mechanical sense. After the war he bought a motor-bike and amused his younger brothers by asking on a very wet day if the rain would 'put the fire out inside'. As a bishop, before the Church Commissioners made it financially possible for diocesans to employ chauffeurs, he had to drive

[1] *Period of my Life*, p.45.

thousands of miles every year in all weathers and, in wartime, in the black-out. Those who drove with him, or watched his departure down a vicarage drive after a service, were generally left with the impression that he had never quite grasped the difference between clutch, gear-lever, and foot-brake. 'Did you drive the Bishop?' someone asked his chaplain at an institution on a particularly foul winter night. 'No,' replied the chaplain mopping his brow, 'the Bishop did the driving, I did the praying.' But if the details of technology were beyond the bishop's understanding, his knowledge of history and human nature which a classical training had afforded him gave him a clear insight into the impact of scientific and tech-nological advance on the mind of man.

What career was Russell to follow? What was he to make of his success in the Schools? He had been elected to a fellowship, then a life-long freehold, at the age of twenty-two. But even if the war had not intervened, it is unlikely that an academic career would have satisfied him for long. Iremonger, in his life of William Temple, wrote 'The Greats School was not meant as a training for professors, scholars and philosophers, it was meant as a training for public life in the Church, at the Bar, in the Civil Service and in Parliament.' Such a conception of education appealed to Russell as it had done to William Temple ten years before.[1] It had not escaped his notice that L. R. Phelps, tutor of Oriel during his day and later provost, and one of the great university characters at the turn of the century, whose obituary Russell was to write in the Oriel *Record* in 1939, was very far from being an inward-looking academic, the fictional absent-minded professor. His interest outside the College was in Poor Law administration and he was a frequent visitor to the Oxford Workhouse, insisting that his pupils, including Russell, should accompany him. He was an object lesson in the correlation of academic prowess and participation in public affairs.

Russell's success in the Schools would have found him a place on the staff of *The Times* and he would soon have become a leader-writer of distinction. Openings were there for the taking. He had not come to Oxford with ordination definitely in mind but the possibility of it was never far from his thoughts. Sometime in his fourth year he made the decision in favour of following his father into the ordained ministry and it was for this reason that he stayed up a fifth year in order to read theology.

V

In his autobiography Russell writes, 'If I am asked why I am a Christian and an Anglican and a parson, the short answer would be, I suppose, "Because my father was".'[2] The short answer, yes—but not the whole answer. His brother, Gerald (eight years younger than himself) who later was to organize the Festival of Britain, shared the same parentage, home and ancestry with him but was neither a believer nor a churchman, although Russell always protested that he had an *anima naturaliter Christiana*. The different courses the two brothers were to take in life can be explained in

[1] After a few years at Queen's as tutor, Temple became a headmaster, a propagandist for church reform and finally a bishop. Outside his own theological and philosophical spheres his interest was in economics.

[2] *Period of my Life,* p.33.

part by the fact that, whereas Russell had a mother's tender care for the first eight years of his life, Gerald never knew his mother because she died in giving him birth. However hard Duncan Barry tried to conceal his feelings, Gerald was probably aware of them, and this may account for a lack of sympathy between father and son. With Russell it was different. Father and son had been linked closely together in the most impressionable years of his life.

Duncan Barry came of an ancient Irish family and boasted that it originated at the Norman Conquest. Russell seldom spoke of his ancestry until he came to write his autobiography and then revealed an unexpected pride in it. His Irishry may account for the romantic streak in his nature and for his propensity for exaggeration in conversation. His father was brought up in the Irish Protestant tradition with its unquestioning acceptance of the verbal inspiration of every word of scripture. At Cambridge he became aware of Biblical criticism then being ventilated in the University by Lightfoot and Westcott. But he remained a conservative in theology and churchmanship and a puritan in personal behaviour till the end of his days.

He did well in the Tripos and was later awarded a B.D. for a thesis on 'The Inspiration and Authority of Holy Scripture'. In his early days he had ambitions for himself as a scholar. It was a great disappointment to him that he was not awarded a D.D. for a book on 'The Ascension of Our Lord'. He was never offered anything more than country benefices and, although he became a Rural Dean, his services were not otherwise recognized. This may be accounted for by the fact that he was suspicious of bishops, expected little of them and certainly never curried favour with them. It sometimes happens that the frustrated hopes of a father affect the ambitions of a son. The careers of the Churchills and the Mountbattens are a case in point. Duncan Barry was at heart a disappointed man, but hurt as he was by the lack of recognition, he never allowed his disappointment to embitter him or to deflect him from his path of duty as a country parson.

At Swanton Morely in Norfolk he raised £8,000—a very considerable sum in those days—to build a new church school even though most of his parishioners were apathetic about the enterprise. He also raised large sums from his friends for the restoration of the vast Norfolk church. He was a highly disciplined and devoted parish priest. Throughout his ministry he said his Office morning and evening in church, he meditated long every morning in his study and his children, waiting impatiently outside, wondered what form these meditations took. He conducted family prayers daily for his family and servants. He took infinite trouble over the services, writing out all the biddings for the prayers in full. His sermons were carefully prepared, rather too long and too erudite for his rural congregation. He had, according to the younger son of the second family, a wonderful presence in church and a fine speaking and singing voice. Year after year he conducted a three-hour service in his own church for a tiny congregation on Good Friday. He was a champion of foreign missions and supported them out of his own pocket, sometimes more generously than he could afford. He was a constant visitor to every home in the parish and he taught weekly in the church school. Yet, at the end of his life, he confessed to one of his children, 'I don't think I have ever had a real experience of the presence of God: it has meant going on in faith, a constant struggle.' His eldest son was to inherit his father's tendency to melancholy and a disposition to court struggle in the inner sanctuaries of faith.

Russell in his later days was inclined to be anxious about his financial position and unashamedly admitted his satisfaction in the royalties that accrued to him from the sale of his books. The poverty of his childhood home made him recognize the value of money. Certainly in the curacy days at Surbiton the Barry family were extremely poor but later in their country parishes they were not so poor as Russell liked to think. Duncan Barry was not without private means and his second wife, according to her younger son, brought with her on marriage quite a handsome dowry. At Denver, the Barrys sat down at their large dining table to a huge sirloin of beef every Sunday and to a leg of mutton in the middle of the week. They kept a cook, two maids, a nanny, a gardener and boy. When Russell made out that conditions in his boyhood were not far removed from those of the Crawley family at Hogglestock Parsonage, he was guilty of exaggeration. Even Mr. Crawley sent a son to Marlborough. Duncan Barry sent his four sons to public schools, admittedly on the scholarships they won for themselves. But the practice of a strict economy at home was essential.

Duncan Barry, as was to be expected, was immensely proud of the brilliant achievements of his eldest son though he became increasingly alarmed by his theological excursions as the years went by. On his visits to his father's home Russell as a young man could be difficult, silent, and provocative, in turn. Arguments between father and son were sometimes heated but a basic confidence between them was never destroyed and, in spite of their theological differences, Russell always acknowledged the debt he owed to his father's example as a priest. He himself would have been far too restless and, for that matter ambitious, to make a good country parson and fortunately was never under pressure to move in that direction, but as a bishop he enjoyed visiting country churches, even though he was not altogether at home in their pulpits. In his last public utterance as Bishop of Southwell, at the Toronto Conference of 1963, he championed the country parson—without doubt with his father's memory in mind.

When Russell went up to Oxford the full force of the Darwinian revolution of the previous century was hitting the University. The new scientific approach which had already been applied to biology, physics and geology was having a more indirect effect upon the interpretation of history and, through history, on theology. Its impact upon the school of philosophy was not to be fully realized at Oxford until the 1930s with the publication of A. J. Ayer's *Language, Truth and Logic*. In Russell's time the philosophic climate was still favourable to a spiritual interpretation of life. The idealistic school which still held the field believed that all branches of knowledge hung together and that there is a pattern running through them discernible to intelligent human inquiry. There was therefore a common ground upon which the philosopher and theologian could stand, even though Oxford philosophy at the turn of the century was less well disposed towards a theology of revelation.

In Oxford theologians were concentrating their attention more on the person of Jesus than on Christology: on his place in history rather than on metaphysics. Hastings Rashdall, a disciple of Harnack, was questioning the miraculous and mysterious element in the New Testament. Then, in 1906, the ascendancy of Harnack on the Continent and Rashdall at Oxford was vigorously assailed by the publication in English of Albert Schweitzer's *The Quest of the Historical Jesus* which had the effect of turning the fashionable historical interpretations of the New Testament upsidedown. It was an exciting time for an intelligent, enquiring young student to turn his attention to the study of theology.

Russell entered into all these controversies with zest and was able to claim blithely fifty years later, when another theological explosion took place shortly after his resignation from the Diocese of Southwell, that he had been through it all before. If ever he found himself out of his depth, like the schoolboy William Temple, he could boast that he could swim. His buoyancy owed much to the spiritual background of his home. He listened to sermons in the University pulpit and was enthralled in particular by the preaching of Winnington-Ingram of whom later he was to become so critical. He had already come to regard theology in terms of exploration rather than of arrival, and would have subscribed to the words of Archbishop Frederick Temple, 'I would say to every honest student in theology: follow the truth, do your utmost to find it and let it be your guide whithersoever it may lead you . . . do not let your study be hampered by a single thought about what the consequences of this or that conclusion may be to you or to others. If it be true, go forward to that truth.'

Russell was ordained by Bishop Gore on the title of his fellowship in Cuddesdon Parish Church in the summer of 1914. He was immensely proud that Gore had ordained him. Years later he was to write, 'Charles Gore, that lovable, enigmatic mixture of authoritarian and free thinker . . . though what Bishop Gore really wanted few people ever understood. I don't think Gore was always right but there are few men for whom I have ever felt a greater reverence.' In his younger days Gore had been considered a radical in his approach to the Bible: in fact had brought down a lot of criticism on his head by his contribution to *Lux Mundi* in 1889. 'That dreadful Mr. Gore that doesn't believe in the Bible.' But now as a diocesan bishop of ten years' standing he seemed to have lost his nerve and to have taken on himself the role of a disciplinarian when his clergy embarked on criticism of the New Testament. Like a game-keeper who had pushed boys to the edge of a plantation he suddenly put up a notice 'Trespassers will be Prosecuted' when they showed some inclination to enter it. Russell's admiration for Gore was profound and there is no doubt that his basic theological orthodoxy owed much to the bishop who accepted him for ordination. At the time candidates for ordination in the Oxford diocese were warned that the bishop had a habit of asking them if they had any doubts, obviously expecting the answer 'no'. No record survives of Russell's interview with the bishop on the eve of his ordination, but it would seem that he left the episcopal study without causing Gore any misgivings.

15

2. ARMAGEDDON

I

Hostilities with Germany broke out within a few weeks of his ordination and Russell stayed on until the middle of 1915 teaching and ministering to an ever-diminishing remnant of undergraduates at Oriel. When the war did not come to an end by the Christmas of 1914, Russell had to make up his mind whether or not to take a more active part in it. As a Liberal in politics he had shared his party's reluctance to accept the inevitability of a European conflagration. By nature he was allergic to the use of violence. Once, in the absence of his parents, he was compelled to administer punishment to his younger half-brother. He laid the erring child across his knees, prepared his seat for judgment, and then could not bring himself to complete the operation. Now he had to wrestle with his conscience before justifying to himself the use of force on a scale hitherto unknown to man.

The fruits of his heartsearching was to appear in the spring of 1915 in a pamphlet justifying the abandonment of a policy of peace. Apart from articles in the college magazine, this pamphlet marks Russell's first appearance in print. It reveals the amount of time that this young man must have spent, while working for his examinations and winning university prizes, in the study of contemporary politics. By the age of twenty-four he had worked out for himself war aims far in advance of most of his contemporaries and elders, 'It is seriously to be hoped,' he wrote, 'that Christian opinion in this country will be strong enough to insist on the return of German colonies and the integrity of her lawful territory and especially ought we to hear nothing of the war on German trade.' The object of the war, he pointed out, was to resist Prussian militarism, not to crush the German peoples for whom he still retained affectionate memories after a short stay at Marburg University, studying theology in 1913. It was at Marburg that he seems to have had a very innocent affair with a young German woman student which did not survive his return to England and the outbreak of war the following year. He now feared that the British Government might take advantage of victory in the pursuit of purely selfish aims by destroying a commercial rival. 'Surely trade [i.e. German as well as British] is a service to the world from a Christian standpoint, not a bait for the avarice of nations.' This is a mature and well-articulated plea for purity of motive and intention in the conduct of war, both of which were soon to be overtaken by a wave of vengeance fostered by the national press.

Having convinced himself that he could now with a clear conscience involve himself more intimately with those who were waging war, Russell advocated a strong line in our resistance to Germany at a time when Haldane was entertaining hopes of a peace settlement. 'To withdraw from this struggle now,' wrote Russell, 'or fight half-heartedly, would be to prolong the war and strengthen the aggressor. The harder we strike, the more merciful the issue . . . when you love a man you may on occasion be compelled to strike him. It is not possible for you to quarrel with him.'

16

In June 1915 while Russell was still kicking his heels in an Oxford which was rapidly being denuded of undergraduates, the Bishop of London, Winnington-Ingram, wrote an article in *The Guardian,* in the manner of St. Bernard arousing Europe for a Crusade, summoning the nation to mobilize for a Holy War. At this period the bishop's activities generally resembled those of a recruiting-sergeant in gaiters. A few weeks later, the archbishops published a Pastoral in the press which included the words, 'The spirit arrayed against us threatens the very foundations of civilized order in Christendom. It can only be rolled back decisively if we for our part concentrate the whole strength of body, mind and soul which our nation and empire holds.' Some Cambridge college chaplains took exception to the implication that it was a Christian's duty to devote his whole strength to the war effort and wrote a very strong letter of protest in *The Guardian* on 11 June accusing the archbishops of apostasy. The poor Archbishop of Canterbury was in a dilemma for, simultaneously, he was being accused by other people of not having written strongly enough in favour of the war effort.

Russell entered the lists with a letter to *The Guardian* on 25 July. He referred briefly to the 'astonishing letter' of the Bishop of London and thanked the Cambridge chaplains for their reply 'which would bring relief to many of us who were pained and bewildered by the expressions of leading churchmen.' He went on, however, to correct an impression that he detected in the Cambridge letter that there was something inconsistent in a priest serving with the forces as a chaplain. 'Surely', he wrote, 'there is no real inconsistency in a man of peace ministering to soldiers. The ordination vow, to set forward as much as in us lieth, quietness, peace and love amongst all Christian people, prevents us from becoming recruiting sergeants but not from helping those who are recruited.' This letter once more reveals maturity in judgment, well in advance of the pronouncements of many of the official leaders of the church at that time. To admit that the Germans and even the Turks and Bulgarians might regard their cause as equally righteous and that, from a divine standpoint, all the belligerants might be equally wrong required great courage in the writer at a time when the press was whipping up hatred against everything German. Before he had actively served as a chaplain and within a month of his being priested, Russell had virtually produced a charter and apologia for the Army Chaplains' Department for all time.

In September 1915, Russell produced his first book, albeit a small one, which he dedicated to those Oriel men who had laid down their lives in the war. In a telling phrase with which readers of his works were later to become so familiar, he wrote ,'The original Austro-Serbian dispute could have been settled at a Sunday luncheon. It was only the existence of colossal armaments behind the lines of every frontier which caused destruction to be let loose.' Again he took the risk of being denounced as pro-German. Perhaps with the young lady in Marburg in mind, he wrote, 'It is well when Zeppelins are hovering over our heads to read some great piece of German writing—realizing the heart-rending imbecility of the present struggle and the essential unity that lies underneath.'

Although the war had only been in progress for ten months and there was as yet no hint of its conclusion, he looks into the future with some foreboding. 'A merely different world is not enough. We must see that it is a better . . . victors will suffer no less than the vanquished.' And what part will the Church play in the building of this new world? Russell thinks that much will depend upon the laity. 'It is they who matter and it is with them that rests the power. Why do not they assert their wishes and force the ministers to put things right?' These words were written two years before William Temple launched the Life and Liberty Movement which included in its programme the bringing of the laity fully into the councils of the Church.

Russell already realized that if Christian doctrine was to mean anything to intelligent people in the twentieth century, it must be communicated in new forms. 'It is no good firing off what is called definite church teaching or "the faith once delivered to the saints" overhead into the air.' As with so many other chaplains this conviction was confirmed in him later when at the Front he came to discover to what an extent the majority of his contemporaries were estranged from the Church.

II

Russell sailed for Egypt with the Rifle Brigade towards the end of 1915 and arrived on the banks of the Canal early in January. Provision for the welfare and entertainment of the troops was far more primitive, where it even existed, in the early part of the first war than it was in the second. As he recounts in his autobiography, his first task was to erect a marquee made out of gas pipes and blankets, as a recreation centre and a place where his services could be held. A soldier who could remember him at this time has written:

> 'After leaving Gallipoli at the end of the evacuation, we had re-equipped at Alexandria and were stationed in the desert at Ismailia to await the next move to the battle-front. Barry was chaplain of the Rifle Brigade who were in camp nearby. We had no chaplain of our own and he invited us to services with his own regiment. He had fixed up a large marquee which acted as a canteen and for his services which I shall never forget. He would stand on the platform and say, very quietly, "This is indeed the House of God, this is the gate of heaven.' The effect was amazing. After a dead silence there was a very real sense of reverential awe in the presence of God.'

In his letter to the dons of Oriel, he admits rather shyly and with characteristic modesty that he who had lived such a protected life hitherto was getting on very well with the troops. 'Tommy is so terribly easy to get on with. He is so fascinatingly desirous—bless him!—of responding to one's efforts on his behalf that he will do anything you tell him.' Russell, as he has to admit in his autobiography, was in danger of becoming a popular parson. In fact, because of his genuine humility, his youthful appearance—so youthful that his Commanding Officer must have wondered who on earth he had been sent as a padre (he was soon to find out)—and his obvious devotion to the welfare of the troops, he was very much loved and soon came to be respected as an influential friend. But all his life, so far from courting popularity, he was positively embarrassed by it.

In his letter to Oriel, he tells more of his activities in Egypt than he records in his autobiography. This letter is a splendid piece of prose, spiced with Latin tags and classical allusions suitable for its recipients, and worthy of a place in some anthology. Apparently he spent much of his time censoring letters and thus learnt more about human nature than he had ever known before. It was he confessed, a pathetic business reading the epistolary efforts of men who had never had to express their feelings to wife or family in writing before. Sometimes he came across complimentary references to himself. One middle-aged soldier wrote to his wife, 'Tell our Elsie [a teen-age daughter] she would be right set up with our young parson.' This flattering reference obviously tickled Russell's fancy. At that time and for years to come, in fact until he fell in love and got engaged at the age of thirty-nine, he showed little interest in girls and was regarded by his friends as a confirmed bachelor.

He describes himself as 'Postman, architect, drayman, philosopher and society entertainer, amanuensis for the illiterate, banker, coffee-stall keeper, lecturer, matrimonial agent, counsel for the defence and— parson.' In the last role Russell took advantage of their station in Bible lands to preach on some of the Old Testament stories. 'It happened over there,' he would say with an expansive gesture of his arms when telling the story of the crossing of the Red Sea. When the C.O. ordered some of the men to make bricks for the cookhouse with inadequate material, the padre reminded him that his behaviour was in the tradition of Pharaoh. 'We have proved the authority of Exodus,' wrote Russell, 'where is the higher criticism now?' It must be borne in mind that in 1916 a very large number of these troops had been in church choirs and attended Bible classes and church day and Sunday schools. Bible stories would be more familiar to them than they would be to this generation.

A sceptical young major in the Manchesters remembers Russell plodding along beside him holding on to the stirrup of his horse, rather breathlessly pouring out arguments in favour of theism. This officer survived the war and was later ordained. When thirty years later the Bishop of Southwell became Chairman of the C.A.C.T.M. Recruitment Committee he knew from long experience what recruitment was about.

It was the human interest that Russell found most absorbing. 'Every hour you make a fresh discovery and have to change your theories on psychology . . . the fascinating thing is to get a man to forget for a moment his regimental number and come forth out of this artificial herding as the real person he was before. If friendship is the only real possession then indeed the chaplain is laying up his treasures.' By the time he was posted to France in June, where the B.E.F. was launched for the attack upon the Somme, he had discovered the true secret of the padre's ministry. But in view of what was in store for him in France, those few months in Egypt in the spring and summer of 1916 must, in retrospect, have seemed like a carefree picnic.

III

The Battle of the Somme opened on 1 July 1916 and on the first day there were 60,000 casualties. Russell as a regimental chaplain attached to the Devons was in the middle of it. By that time, padres had won their way into the front line after initial resistance from many commanding officers. In *Period of my Life,* he has given the outline of his activities in the trenches. But no autobiographer, let alone Russell, would ever bring himself to allude to his own valour. He in fact did the reverse. The nearest he gets to mentioning his own reputation for courage is in the words, 'They thought I was brave' and then quickly seems to dismiss the suggestion by dwelling on how terribly afraid he was. The hero, of course, is not the man who knows no fear, but the sensitive and imaginative man who is afraid and yet overcomes his fear, as Russell did. An old friend once asked him why he was awarded the D.S.O. and got the answer with the characteristic shrug of the shoulders, 'I happened to be the last one out of a dug-out', which seems to be a *non sequitur*. On the day he got engaged on the Berkshire Downs, his fiancée asked the same question. This time he was a little more explicit. 'Oh, for doing a little first-aid in No Man's Land.' He never referred to the subject again nor did he ever mention it apparently to anyone in later years that he had sat up all night with a soldier sentenced to be shot for cowardice the following morning. There could hardly be a more harrowing experience than this. Yet when he was appointed to the diocese of South-well, there were those who said he was lacking in pastoral experience. The Citation for his D.S.O. ran as follows:

> 'He tended and dressed the wounded under very heavy fire with the greatest courage and determination. He set a splendid example throughout the operation.'

They thought he was brave because he *was* brave. It was said at the time that he was recommended for the V.C. and was not awarded it because two other Church of England chaplains had been given it that year.

In an article at that time quoting from the Gospel text, 'Jesus looking on him, loved him' Russell adds, 'I imagine him as one of our boy lance-corporals, full of laughter and glorious instincts, exactly the kind of boy that Jesus wanted.' There is no doubt that Russell gave himself to the troops and later to the students at Knutsford in a way which he could not bring himself to recapture later in life. How can we account for the fact that the soldier in the trenches touched Russell deeper down in his being than anyone else, apart from his family, was able to do after the war? An incumbent in his diocese later thought he had the answer. Russell had been deprived of a mother's love in childhood. In the trenches he was ministering to young men who were also deprived of all feminine attention. Just as wounded soldiers in the Middle Ages cried out in their agony to the Mother of Christ, so would soldiers in Flanders in their delirium cry out for their mothers. Out in No Man's Land, Russell extended a mother's care to what he regarded as his hurt children. The little boy who had cried himself to sleep night after night at school had a natural sympathy with them.

In September 1917, after Russell had been promoted to be senior chaplain of a Division and was by comparison with July 1916 a little more with-drawn from the front line, he was invited by the Rev. E. B. Macnutt to contribute along with several other army chaplains to a symposium which was published under the title *Church in the Furnace* which Barry nick-named 'Fat in the Fire'. Among the other contributors were Linton Smith, later Bishop of Rochester, Milner White, later Dean of York, C. S. Woodward, later Bishop of Bristol and Gloucester, E. S. Woods, later Bishop of Lichfield, Neville Talbot who as a retired overseas bishop was to be Vicar of St. Mary's, Nottingham when Russell went to Southwell, and G. A. Studdert-Kennedy, perhaps the best-known army padre of the war.

His own article, entitled, 'Faith in the Light of War', gives the most vivid description of the effect of the fighting of the year before upon him.

> 'After the fighting on the Somme on 26 September, 1916, worn out and atheistic, and incapable of prayer, I began glancing at my Prayer Book. I shall never forget the rush of light that came with the Michaelmas Epistle.[1] It is untrue that war is a reviver of religion. It is for myself a constant struggle to keep the spiritual sense alive at all. A life that varies between impersonal monotony and un-nameable obscenity with never any privacy, leisure, or comfort, is not very fruitful soil in which to seek for new growth of spiritual power. Every spark of glamour and romance has disappeared from warfare long ago. It is just an orgy of monotony.'

And then he breaks off to describe the refreshment he derived from nature which even intensive bombardment could not destroy.

> 'The clouds and sunsets are still sacramental. The poppies on the way up to the trenches, the primrose in the deserted garden when we get back "are very full of divinity" for us. They help us to realize that, after all, the sane and beautiful endure untouched by the passing madness of men.'

This passage reveals very much of the inner man of Russell: his candour, his vulnerability, his reliance on the daily office, and the part that nature played in support of his faith.

Further on in this article, Russell disproved his tutor's forecast that he would forget all that he had learnt in reading for Greats. 'Faith is autonomous: a genuine faculty of knowledge submitting to no test outside itself', he wrote, quoting Kant. In later years some of his clergy may have interpreted his reluctance to conduct retreats and quiet days and his refusal to attend them as suggesting that his faith was largely cerebral. This was quite untrue. There was a strong streak of emotion in it kept carefully under control: 'What we need is a faith that is bold enough to state essential things essentially.'

Even though he wrote in the middle of the Passchendaele disaster and the future of the war was still not predictable, Russell was looking ahead to the days after the war and, like so many other chaplains, to the part which the church would play in reconstruction.

> 'We are so choked by accumulations, so occupied with trivialities. The Church has specialized in irrelevancies ... no padre, certainly, and

[1] Revelation 12: 'And there was war in heaven: Michael and his angels fought against the dragon; and the dragon fought and his angels, and prevailed not ... and I heard a loud voice saying in heaven, Now is come salvation, and strength, and the kingdom of our God, and the power of his Christ.'

probably no man can find rest for his soul when the war is over in the religion of parochial activities . . . I am quite prepared to see such large developments in the coming form of Christianity that the religion of our sons and grandsons would seem almost another faith if they were witnessed by their grandfathers.'

But he was not over-optimistic:

'Yet, candidly, it is to me in some moods the thing I dread and shrink from most of all. It is not only the inevitable reaction in the nation as a whole, it is for the very boys that one loves in France and longs to see released from this hateful life. What for them is the moral and religious future? Certainly everything depends on the atmosphere to which they return.'

Prophetic words indeed. With hindsight, we can now compare Russell's premonitions in 1917 with the actual aftermath of war: the newly elected House of Commons of 1919 with its 'hard-faced men who looked as if they had done well out of the war': the queues for the dole, the hunger marches, and the General Strike of 1926.

Very few veterans of the first world war who knew Russell at that time have survived. One who served under him in the Division and later succeeded him as senior chaplain wrote:

'I remember him going up to the Canal bank the night before Passchendaele and celebrating communion for the chaplains whose units were involved. I know we thought that chaplains' meetings with him were inspiring and though intellectually he was far above most of us, he never made any of us feel inferior . . . Incidentally, in his mess at Divisional H.O. officers looked forward to discussions in which he and the R.C. chaplain, a Jesuit, took part.'

Another voice comes to us from across the years. This from a retired Colonel who, as a young Captain, was keeping a diary:

'On Sundays we went to the service in the Church Army hut. These services were always taken by the Divisional Chaplain, Major [sic] Barry D.S.O., a very popular officer.'

And later:

'Just before the battle of Cambrai on Sunday we went to the Church Army hut where Major Barry, C.F., preached about the attack we were going to take part in and after the service most of us stayed for communion.'

The next day many of those communicants were dead.

Many chaplains in the war were brave, some were popular, but only a few were men of intellectual distinction. Even fewer combined all these qualities and of these Russell was one. Yet after the war, he seldom referred to his wartime experiences—unlike the archdeacon of whom it was said in September 1939 'The only good thing that can be said about the outbreak of this war is that it will stop the archdeacon talking about the last.' He never flaunted his medals, nor was he a conspicuous figure at Remembrance Day celebrations. The war was too distasteful a subject for him to dwell upon, even in private.

There were chaplains who made names for themselves under wartime conditions and never really recovered from the outbreak of peace, whose ministry as a consequence was always something of an anti-climax. This was certainly not the case with Russell. The war had deepened him and brought out gifts hitherto unsuspected largely because, on account of his youth, he had had no time previously to display them. It refined his faith. As we have seen all the way through, even in the darkest days he had been looking into the future, sometimes with optimism, sometimes taking on the role of a Jeremiah. Now he was entering that future upon which he had bestowed so much thought. He was soon to be given an opportunity to play an important part in the attempt at reconstruction.

IV

In the last months of the war, Russell had been promoted by Bishop Gwynne, the deputy Chaplain-General, B.E.F., to the post of Assistant Chaplain-General, carrying with it the rank of Lieutenant-Colonel. This was promotion indeed. Heavy casualties in France had given young officers in their twenties unexpected opportunities for promotion to staff rank. The casualties proportionately were not so heavy amongst padres and, as a result, very few of them reached the rank of Senior Chaplain, certainly not under the age of thirty. Promotion meant that Russell was further withdrawn from the front line and this he deeply regretted, but it did give him his first experience of ministering to other clergymen, an experience which was to prove invaluable to him in the future. Bishop Gwynne set Russell's feet on the rung of a ladder which was to raise him eventually to the Bench of Bishops, and right away from a purely academic career to which at that moment he may have been expecting to return on the cessation of hostilities.

During the war many young men in all three services had felt a vocation to ordination. The war had had the effect of undermining the faith of some while fostering it in others. Many of the latter had spoken to their padres and in many cases their names had been jotted down in diaries and notebooks. Tubby Clayton had collected a fairly comprehensive list at Toc H. Some of them had a pre-war university experience behind them, a few had already embarked on theological training before they enlisted. The faith of all of them had taken a battering. They were spiritually shocked, restless, and along with many of the chaplains, highly critical of the Church, which for many of them was the chief barrier to ordination. There was also another barrier. Hitherto, bishops had insisted on a university degree before a man was accepted for ordination, a requirement which had the effect of blocking the way for nearly all men whose fathers could not afford further education for their sons. The Church had been content to recruit for the ministry almost exclusively from the upper and middle classes. In 1918 many servicemen with a vocation had nothing apart from the promised gratuity to cover the cost of training.

In the first few weeks after the fighting ended, the War Office realized that something must be done to keep the troops quiet. The provision of 'bread and circuses' was not enough. Plans were made for widespread schemes of education to occupy the spare time of the troops and to prepare them for the transfer to 'civvy street'. Bishop Gwynne wholeheartedly fell in with this plan as far as would-be ordinands were concerned. A hutted machine-gun camp at Le Touquet was converted for this purpose. Then came the more difficult task of finding exactly the right man to run it. The first intake would still be under military discipline. This meant that it had to have a combatant officer nominally in charge, while the real principal was given the title of Chief Education Officer. For this delicate task it is not surprising that the bishop's choice fell upon Russell who was then approaching his twenty-ninth birthday.

Russell himself tells the story of the test school in his autobiography and it has been told elsewhere, so it need not be repeated in detail here. It was a crucial moment in the history of ordination training in the Church of England. Archbishop Davidson who had previously been severely criticized by some of the more radical of the army chaplains visited the school and not only won the respect of the men, but left behind him his famous pledge that those who were recommended for training should never have to call it off for lack of funds. It was during this visit that a warm friendship was struck up between the aged Archbishop and Russell in spite of differences of age and temperament. It was to be revived a few years later when Russell's friend, Mervyn Haigh, became Chaplain at Lambeth.[1]

The test school at Le Touquet not only initiated a new principle in theological education but was also, as Russell claimed, the first College of Education of its kind. While the proposed scheme of army education was still being debated elsewhere and had not got further than plans on paper, Russell went ahead with furnishing, equipping, and then opening, his school. In the few months of its existence the Board of Education reported enthusiastically on its work. Russell wrote, 'Whitehall may have learnt something from the Church.' To his way of thinking the Church was there to educate, enlighten and enrich public opinion. As William Temple was to say, 'The Church is the only voluntary society which exists primarily for non-members.'

V

To those men who were herded into the hutted camp it was the warmth of the welcome they received from the 'Chief' which impressed them most. For months or years they had been under military discipline. Even the method of recruiting them was true to type. One soldier remembers a regimental

---

1 Russell's previous criticisms of the Archbishop and the episcopate generally had occasioned Bishop Gwynne's jibe one morning before a service when Russell was helping him on with his robes, 'You are better at dressing bishops down than dressing them up.'

Later Russell was to write of Davidson:

'I can never think without reverence and affection of that great old man, so wise and generous, who admitted me and other members of my age to a confidence which we had no right to expect. He was not what would be called a leader. He may have carried his innate reluctance to commit himself to decisions too far—to the point of an occupational disease—but his legacy was that he left the door open and thus enabled great things to happen.'

parade in the Army of Occupation near Cologne. The Sergeant-major shouted, 'All men who want to be clergymen in the Church of England, one step forward march.' Courageously, this man took a step forward, the first on his way to Le Touquet. A corporal in the Brigade of Guards describes the procedure which brought him there:

'One day I got a great surprise. During one of the ten-minute halts, the Company Captain came to our section and called for me. I had never spoken to him before: Guards discipline did not allow rankers being on speaking terms with commissioned officers and so I was greatly surprised when he asked, "Corporal, have you ever thought of taking orders in the Church of England?" I had no difficulty in answering "Yes Sir," "Think about it," said the Captain, "and let me have a definite answer in a few days." . . . After a few more days a chaplain came to see me . . . then things began to move. I was given a railway voucher and told to go to Duren. There, along with several other prospective ordinands, I appeared before a formidable Board of Army chaplains. In spite of my fears and nervousness the interview was pleasant and back I went to the mob. Within a few days I was called up to the Company Office and given a railway voucher and told to proceed to the Ordination Test Centre, Le Touquet, France. It was January and there was a lot of snow on the ground. The cattle trucks in which we travelled were far from weatherproof. We were not given any food, but one of our fellow travellers was a commissioned officer and from time to time he managed to scrounge something for us to eat. We collected snow in our billy cans, and when we had enough water to make tea we managed to get it boiled on coals which the engine-driver kindly gave us.

'At last we arrived at Le Touquet and went to the office to report. There I got a most welcome surprise. Seated behind a desk was a chaplain with the insignia of a colonel on his shoulder. As soon as he saw us he jumped up with a happy smile and came to us with outstretched hand and greeted us most warmly. He enquired about our well-being, were we hungry, etc. and then said, "Come on, boys, I'll show you to your hut." What a happy change from being nothing but a number to being treated as a friend. That was my first meeting with F.R.B. and the memory of it is still pleasantly vivid.'

All the survivors from the Le Touquet School remember Russell's talks on the New Testament to which they listened enthralled in spite of the cold of the winter of 1918-19. One old pupil wrote:

'My earliest recollection of you, Chief, is in the dining hall at Le Touquet at 9.30 a.m. I can see you now striding up and down before that khaki crowd with a row of chaplains in front and pouring forth about the prophets. It was then, I think, that I first realized that they could mean something. I don't know what you did without the sleeve of your gown to play with. [This in reference to a familiar mannerism which Russell was to adopt later when lecturing in an M.A. gown.] I rather fancy you used the ends of that big woolly muffler with which you swathed your neck, for it was passing cold in those days.'

A photograph taken in January 1919 shows Russell in a Norfolk jacket, an article of clothing which was just going out of fashion, knee breeches and thick stockings. He is still very youthful in appearance, so youthful that were it not for the clerical collar, he might be taken for an undergraduate. There are no obvious signs of the strain of war in his face. At a tennis party in Knutsford that spring when everyone was talking about the great Mr. Barry, a lady approached him and asked, 'Are you Mr. Barry's son?' 'Yes,' replied Russell truthfully. 'Then where is your father?' she asked. Some of his friends have described Russell's countenance as simian. That may be so: but there is a singular beauty in its expression, an intensity in the eyes, but humour lurks about the mouth.

It was clear from the start that the Le Touquet experiment would be only temporary. It could last only as long as there were servicemen on the Continent seeking to be ordained. Tubby Clayton was therefore commissioned to return to the United Kingdom to look for civilian accommodation. An official of the Ministry of Housing warned that large empty houses were in short supply. 'I can only offer you a prison,' he added laughingly. 'Show me one,' replied Tubby unexpectedly. Together they journeyed to Cheshire where Tubby immediately accepted the disused prison at Knutsford. The whole episode appealed to his sense of humour as it did to the men at Le Touquet when he returned with the news. A former student remembers that they 'rocked and rolled' with laughter and a wag pinned on the notice board a Temperance poster depicting a convict in a prison cell, carrying the caption, 'What has brought him to this?' under which was scrawled, 'The Church of England!' Still, even a disused prison was to prove more comfortable than a hutted military camp at Le Touquet. It had been a hard winter on the Channel coast which the warmth of the 'Chief's' welcome, and his high spirits, coupled with the challenge of his daily address at 9.30, had helped the inmates to ignore. In those two months Russell had accepted the kind of challenge which always fired his blood.

VI

What was Russell's specific contribution to the Church and the forwarding of the Christian faith through his three years' service as an Army Chaplain? As a padre in the battlezone he had been outstandingly effective. Many soldiers died more peacefully because of his last-minute ministrations in the trenches; many must have survived their wounds who otherwise would not have done so, without his first aid in No Man's Land. Thousands must have been strengthened in their faith by his addresses at improvised services behind the lines and by casual conversations in dugouts at the front. Later on he gave, as Senior Chaplain, great encouragement to his juniors many of whom were to hold positions of responsibility in the Church after the war. At the same time he reached out during those three years to a wider public at home through his letters to the press.

Russell's moderation in his attitude towards the enemy and his refusal to identify the cause of the Allies with that of the Kingdom of God, did much to counterbalance the warlike utterances of prominent clerics like Winnington-Ingram which were widely reported in the press and gave great offence to thinking people. Both Russell and Studdert-Kennedy delved much deeper. Their experiences on the Somme in July 1916 certainly had a deep effect on their yet unmatured theology. Both felt instinctively that the transcendent impassible God, which Neoplatonism had fastened on Christian orthodoxy in the third and fourth centuries, would never commend the gospel to an increasingly sceptical public. A God utterly unmoved by the sufferings of his children just would not do. Many years later Russell was to write that Hellenistic Christianity 'found it difficult to accept Christ as God if he suffered.' 'This generation,' Russell commented, 'would find it difficult if he didn't.' This shift of emphasis towards a more immanent, sharing, deity which Russell and Geoffrey Studdert-Kennedy adopted in 1916 and was not without its dangers, found its way into the lifeblood of Christian thinking in the years that lay ahead.[1]

Along with other chaplains who served in France, Russell underwent a shattering disillusionment with the institutional church. Although he later deplored the rudeness of Harry Blackburne[2] to the Archbishop of Canterbury when he visited the B.E.F. in 1916, he contributed his fair share of criticisms of the Church. It had been brought home to the chaplains, face to face with common humanity as never before, just how wide a gap existed between the clergy and the man in the street, now turned man in the trenches; and for that matter between the man in the pulpit and the man in the pew of which there were many more in 1914 than today. Amongst other things, the chaplains came to realize how very upper and middle class the leadership of the Church was. Convinced that the Church needed re-handling from top to bottom, the chaplains in the field returned home in 1919 with a sense of social guilt and a dis-satisfaction with things as they were which were to characterize the state of mind of many of the clergy for the next two generations. When, fifty years later, Russell accused the younger clergy of a loss of nerve and a tendency to surrender strongholds before they were invested, it may have escaped his notice that he and many other army chaplains of the First World War were in part responsible for injecting the clergy of the future with a restlessness of which later, as retired bishop, he became critical.

Perhaps Russell's greatest contribution to the war years and to their aftermath was the encouragement he gave to war-weary and shaken chaplains, as well as to serving soldiers who were offering themselves for ordination: the men who were to be manning the parishes in the thirties, forties and fifties. Later he was able to inspire all the more effectively because, unlike many other highly successful chaplains, he never gave the impression that he had reached heights in the war years from which subsequently he dropped. Nor, like distinguished chaplains such as Eric Milner-White and Kenneth Kirk did he retreat from war-time radicalism into a narrow ecclesiastical embrasure as soon as hostilities ceased. The war was over. It had deepened his faith and profoundly affected his way of thinking. His eyes were now fixed on the future.

[1] See Alan Wilkinson *The Church of England in the First World War,* p.246.
[2] later Dean of Bristol.

3. RESURGAM

The staff and students migrated from France to Cheshire in February 1919 where they were shortly joined by others who had not been to Le Touquet. It was Russell's intention to provide, through the inspiration of the school, future clergy of the calibre and quality to make the Enabling Act of 1919 work in the parishes. More than that, as Knutsford was not strictly speaking a theological college in the specialist sense of that term, but a test and pre-training school for men with ordination in mind, he wanted to make it a model for adult education throughout the country. He was never content with the church training its members in churchery as the medievals had done. But, unlike some other teachers and trainers with high ambitions for the church, he never tried to force the pupils into a preconceived mould or pattern. He cared for the men as individuals far too much to make that mistake.

Around himself Russell gathered a very strong staff: probably no stronger staff existed in any educational establishment beneath the level of the Universities at that time. Mervyn Haigh, his closest friend, later to become Bishop of Coventry and then of Winchester, had one of the ablest brains in the Church. He was a reserved, rather austere, man and provided an excellent foil for Russell. Once at a tennis party, the child of the family addressed Mervyn. 'Man, get my ball out of those bushes.' Mervyn instanty complied. 'Good heavens,' said Russell, 'I have never heard anyone give Mervyn an order before and what is more, it was instantly obeyed!' Mervyn and Russell had a warm mutual regard for each other and later Mervyn confessed that he could never speak of Knutsford without becoming lyrical.

R. V. H. Burne, later Archdeacon of Chester, 'Burno' or 'the Bish' to the students, was Senior Tutor, responsible for the syllabus and the tricky task of arranging the lecturing in a building not designed for the purpose. He was scholarly, capable and utterly reliable and was later to succeed Russell as principal. In a course of addresses on Christian love, after Russell and Mervyn Haigh had risen to great spiritual heights and held their audience spellbound, Burne, speaking third, brought them all down to earth by beginning, 'I will tell you what Christian love really is. It is not taking more than four inches of bath water.' The inmates of the prison who had experienced the lack of water in the taps were in a good position to appreciate this sound piece of theological advice.

'Tubby Clayton, whose brainchild the Knutsford Test School had been, was a frequent visitor, always welcome for his rollicking and quite irrepressible fun. His absences grew longer when he began to travel the country translating Toc H from wartime to peacetime conditions. He soon became a national figure. Geoffrey Heawood, later the highly respected and greatly loved headmaster of Cheltenham Grammar School, and after that lay Secretary of C.A.C.T.M., was a tutor. F. M. Sykes, 'Syko' to the troops when he was a very popular army chaplain, and 'Psycho' to the school, concentrated on pastoralia. Reputedly an Anglo-catholic, it was to him Russell turned over the students who found the general tenor of the school too liberal. He was a big, jolly, loving man and was greatly missed when he was taken away to become Vicar of Middlesborough.

The School opened with Evensong in the parish church of Knutsford which served as a chapel. The prison chapel was deemed too gloomy for the purpose. It was an occasion which those who participated in it never forgot. The singing of Psalm 126,

'When the Lord turned again the captivity of Zion,
then were we like unto them that dream.
Then was our mouth filled with laughter:
and our tongue with joy',

exactly matched the mood of the congregation. Russell spoke eloquently of being 'gathered together out of the heart of a great tragedy into the heart of a great opportunity.' The moment for which he had been looking forward for nearly five years had come. In a practical way, concentrated within the walls of the gaol at Knutsford was all the emotion and resolve symbolized by the gatherings around village War Memorials and the annual Remembrance services at the Cenotaph and in the Albert Hall.

There was much fun and fooling at Knutsford. Russell, whose deafness, though already marked, had not raised a barrier between himself and other people, was always in the middle of it. He played tennis and went for cross-country runs. In the common room, where once convicts had worked away on mailbags, they played charades and 'Nebuchadnezzar'. On one occasion the lights were turned out and outer darkness reigned, until Russell flashed a torch on to Tubby in the role of Archimedes, stark naked in a hip-bath of the sort which used to be kept under beds. Russell was the life and soul of the Sunday evening informal discussions in a smoke-filled room, serious and rollicking by turns, making the kind of quips about the Church and clergymen which had already become a characteristic part of his repertoire. A student of those days remembers the queer little chuckles and swallowings and the thrusting forward of the chin which preceded the more outrageous of his sallies followed by a flick of the tongue to signify the same kind of satisfaction as a tennis star might feel after getting a fast one in down the side line. These mannerisms were to win the hearts of people who might otherwise have been shocked by his racy conversation. 'I have never come across such a measure of fun, gaiety and seriousness which he so generously shared with us', one of his students has written.

But what impressed the students more than anything else was Russell's morning Bible readings. In these he made the characters and episodes in the Old and New Testaments really come alive and then applied them to situations which the students might encounter in the future. The slight figure on the platform, seemingly tearing itself apart, twisting the sleeves of the M.A. gown, which replaced the Le Touquet muffler, into knots and rattling coins in his pocket, were a lifetime memory to those who heard him. 'Magnetic', 'dynamic', are words which even the restrained Mervyn Haigh was ready to apply to him.

During the time that the school was at the gaol 900 men passed through it. The maximum number at any one time was 350. Russell from the beginning realized that in the nature of things the school had a *terminus ad quem*. It could only continue in its present form while there were still candidates for ordination amongst the war veterans. By the end of 1922, membership was down to 93 and Russell was beginning to take young men straight from civilian life. It was this that convinced him that the Church must open the doors of the ordained ministry to a wider intake than hitherto and that Knutsford must continue in some form either there or elsewhere as a permanent feature of pre-theological training. The fact that under him the school had been such a resounding success made his vision all the more acceptable to the authorities. In October 1922 the school moved to a private house called 'Kilrie' in Knutsford and a month later Russell announced that he was on the move.

Russell was proud of his achievement, particularly of having established the principle that men of all walks of life might be enabled to train for the ministry. But many years later in an address to the old students he admitted to second thoughts about the advisability of opening the gates so wide. Was it a good thing that a majority of the clergy in the Church of England should be non-graduates when, as Russell put it with characteristic pungency, 'Every woodwork instructor has a degree'? After becoming a bishop, he came to the conclusion that the parish clergy would never be effective if they could not out-think the majority of their parishioners. Some people thought his emphasis on intellectual qualification was excessive.

To understand the Knutsford period and the part it played in Russell's life we must realize that the end of the war took people in two ways. There were those who were intent on making up for the years lost by having a good time at all costs. There were others, perhaps a minority, who were committed to building a new and better world. In this category there were politicians like Anthony Eden, Clement Attlee and Harold Macmillan, all of them ex-officers. Amongst the padres there were men like P. B. Clayton, Geoffrey Studdert-Kennedy and F. R. Barry. For them there could not be, or at least there must not be, another war and the best way of preventing one was to remove the causes. None of them in those days doubted that the British Empire had a big part to play in the creation of a new world. They were buoyed up with a confident sense of mission such as this generation conspicuously lacks. Russell in his old age was conscious of a wide gulf between his contemporaries and the rising generation. It is highly improbable that he ever heard young people talking about 'your boring old war' as he states in *Period of my Life*. This typical bit of Barryan exaggeration was his way of admitting that young people in the 1970s could never really recapture the sense of dedication, high hopes and enthusiasm, with which he and his friends at Knutsford emerged from the First World War.

One feature of the society at Knutsford must strike the younger generation today as particularly odd and that is the lack of any feminine element there. Except for a detachment of W.A.C.s, still under military discipline, who did the cooking for the students and kept themselves to the cookhouse, the students never saw a woman within the walls of the prison. They themselves made the beds and waited at table. Those who had been educated at public schools and the universities had already been conditioned to living in an exclusively male environment. Russell in his autobiography speaks of the precautions that were taken at Oxford to prevent any young woman entering a college without a chaperone. Then came the war. Life in the forward areas was starkly masculine. The wounded were, of course, tended by nurses not far behind the lines but strict hospital discipline discouraged the nurses from having anything but the most fleeting personal relationships with their patients. Of course a large number of men found girls for casual sexual indulgence in French and Belgian towns and villages when, for short periods, they came out of the line.

It would have been expected, therefore, that when the war came to an end, the prospect of female companionship would be one of the main attractions that peace had to offer. For the majority of men it was. What is remarkable is that the staff and students at Knutsford were so ready to continue in their bachelor state, as far as many of the students were concerned, right on into their curacy days as well. Of the staff, Barry, who was at that time wrongly supposed to be a misogynist, did not marry until his fortieth year: Burne married in middle life. Tubby Clayton and Mervyn Haigh remained permanent bachelors.

A college life without feminine companionship is almost unimaginable today when co-educational establishments are the fashion at all age levels, and women are invading what were once regarded as the most impregnable masculine citadels. It is generally assumed that a student cannot attend to his or her studies without the society of the opposite sex. But even after the Second World War, some old-fashioned dons still continued to deplore the presence of women in the universities. 'The women spoil the chances of my young men in their first year by getting engaged to them and again in their third year by breaking the engagement off,' one elderly tutor complained.

There were of course, homosexual groups in the universities and in London society at the turn of the century, and today we are hearing more and more about them. But the majority of students, particularly those who were preparing to serve the country and Empire as teachers and administrators, lived cheerfully and contentedly together for long periods in an exclusively male society and enjoyed warm friendships which had no suggestion of homosexual leanings. The present generation must find this incredible. But fifty years ago boys at public schools were encouraged to regard those of their own sex who preferred the company of girls to the fellowship of the football field as degenerate. It was taken for granted that in the learned professions a marriage before twenty-eight would be the exception. In the Church this was certainly the case. Some bishops would not allow ordinands to embark on marriage within three years of ordination. 'You cannot embrace two vocations at once,' Archbishop William Temple advised his ordination candidates. The Empire still loomed large in the career prospects of the ablest boys and young men in public schools and universities and the prospect of service to the Empire made postponement of marriage inevitable, and seems to have rendered temporary celibacy endurable. This may explain how the staff and students at Knutsford succeeded in living together cheerfully and healthily without feminine companionship.

4. STRANGE INTERLUDE

I

In the summer of 1923 after an interval of seven years Russell found himself back in Egypt once more. His acceptance of the archdeaconry in Cairo was a surprise to his friends and was actually opposed by the Archbishop of Canterbury, Randall Davidson. The Archbishop told him that more important work would open up for him at home, without exactly specifying what it was likely to be. Bishop Gwynne who had returned to Egypt after the war was equally pressing in the opposite direction. He had been Russell's chief in France. It was he who had rescued the Army Chaplain's Department from the low state into which it had fallen at the beginning of the war. He had shown a special interest in Russell whom he regarded as one of the brightest of his chaplains and Russell responded with affection bordering on hero-worship. He was in a difficult position. Then, just before he was due to sail, the post of Professor of New Testament Studies at King's College, London, fell vacant and the Archbishop urged him to put in for it. It is unusual for a young clergyman to accept a post overseas and simultaneously to apply for another at home. Russell considered his chances of being offered the professorship so remote that he took the risk.

If an archdeaconry on the Nile was anything like one in England then Russell was quite unsuited for it. Bishop Gwynne had made no attempt to describe the work that would be expected of him. On arrival in Cairo he found that the bishop had returned on leave to England, so he was left guessing for two or three months what the job entailed. In that time he made some new friends, including that great missionary Temple Gairdner with whom he went camping in the desert near the Pyramids. He had lunch with the British Resident and his wife. Field-Marshal Allenby made it quite clear that he was not interested in young clergymen, obviously not realizing that Russell was an exceptional one. He rose from the table and left the room before the end of the meal. Lady Allenby was herself a parson's daughter and, as Russell put it in his autobiography, 'knew what to say.' Years later, as canon of Westminster, he looked back to this incident with amusement when it fell to him to bury the Field-Marshal's ashes in the Abbey.[1] When Bishop Gwynne returned to the diocese it was to tell his new archdeacon, with whom he had not yet worked, that under pressure from the Archbishop he would release him for the post at King's.

Russell was always grateful for this curious interlude in his career. It gave him the opportunity of visiting the Holy Land and of observing the British Empire in action at close quarters. Bishop Gwynne was on intimate terms with the Egypt and Sudan political Civil Service, whose members were carefully picked from the elite of Oxford and Cambridge graduates. He was frequently consulted by officials from the Resident downwards. As we have seen, Russell had unqualified admiration for his old chief even though he was not unaware of his shortcomings and disagreed with his archaic political opinions. There could not have been a greater contrast between the two men. Gwynne had been 'capped' for Wales in his young days and as a curate in Nottingham had played as an amateur for Notting-

---

[1] Later still, when he was Bishop of Southwell, he chose as his chaplain another Allenby, a distant relation of the great soldier.

ham Forest. His vicar's son, Edward Woods, later Bishop of Lichfield, described him as he remembered him in his boyhood as a perfect example of a 'two-fisted he-man'. He was no intellectual but the absence of subtle thinking has often been an advantage to overseas clergy when dealing with men of action in high places.

When Russell was in Egypt the cathedral which became so well known to thousands of men of the Eighth Army had not yet been built. During the Second World War it gave him some satisfaction to recall that in the few months he had spent in Cairo he had set in motion the selling of the original Anglican cathedral, a very unworthy building, and the raising of the money to provide a new one.

II

The invitation to be Professor of New Testament Studies in King's College, London, was attractive to Russell largely because he thoroughly approved of the status of the divinity faculty within the university. He had not much enjoyed his one term in the Barchester setting of Wells Theological College, regarding the nineteenth century policy of planting theological colleges either in cathedral cities or in remote country districts as a step in the wrong direction. As W. R. Matthews, his colleague at King's, was to write, 'In my opinion, isolated theological colleges though often wonderful schools of the spiritual life, have been on the whole mistakenly aloof from the world.' Russell shared Matthews's allergy to the seminary. But King's was different. The theological faculty was originally part of a college which embraced other disciplines; and King's, though originally an Anglican foundation, was part of the greater university of London which in origin had been decidedly secular in tone and purpose. King's was governed by a lay principal, not necessarily an Anglican. In Russell's day it was the great classicist Ernest Barker. Walter Matthews presided over the divinity faculty and was a man after Russell's own heart. The divinity staff shared a common room with the fellows of other departments. The theological students played their part in the university union. After he had retired from the deanery of St. Paul's, Matthews was to write in his autobiography, 'The room in which I normally lectured was in my time uncomfortably close to a chemical laboratory which now and then emitted penetrating odours of H_2SO_4. I remember saying to a restive audience of theologians: "Perhaps these fumes are a device of Satan to prevent you from attending to my words of wisdom, but it is equally likely that they are meant by Providence to remind us that we must always take account of scientific methods and truth." [1] Like Matthews, Russell was happiest doing theology within a secular context. Years later when he was a bishop, he defended his decision to hold a clergy school in the high season at a Butlins camp against the complaints of some of his clergy.

Russell obviously brought a breath of fresh air to the College, not only by the actual content of his lectures but by his general demeanour in the classrooms and corridors. One old student remembers his first appearance as a lecturer. His entry into the classroom was heralded by an Oxford M.A. gown flying through the door in the direction of the rostrum, to be followed a second later by the lecturer himself. 'That's better,' he said, 'now we can

[1] W. R. Matthews *Memories and Meanings* (Hodder, 1969) p.115.

get down to it.' Russell was given a set of rooms in the college hostel in Vincent Square and after a time became Warden. He was responsible for discipline which then, as always, he found irksome. But any barrier which the enforcement of rules might have erected between him and his students was offset by such notices as the one that appeared in the bathroom next to his bedroom, as a plea to those students who performed their ablutions after returning home in the small hours, 'From things that go bump in the night, good Lord, deliver us.'

King's provided courses of lectures in the evening for men and women who were in full-time employment, with the result that Russell found himself working by night as well as by day. More and more he was being drawn into activities outside the College. He was on intimate terms with most of the coming young men in the Church. Mervyn Haigh was at Lambeth and they often had walks together at Richmond on Saturday afternoons. Largely through Haigh's influence, he was invited to be a member of the Archbishop's Commission on Doctrine in 1923. He was only thirty-three years of age and by far the youngest member. It was said that the Archbishop realized that he was sentencing the distinguished scholars who composed the Commission to many years' hard labour and wanted to ensure that at least a few would survive until the report was finally published. In the event it did not see the light of day until 1938 and Russell survived its publication by nearly forty years. It was overshadowed by the outbreak of the Second World War and when the Church was able to give its attention to it again, the whole theological climate had changed. But at least it ensured that in future ordained theologians who questioned the historicity of the Virgin Birth would not be prosecuted for heresy.

Russell was also invited to join an informal group of able young parsons, all of whom had seen war service and were anxious to bring pressure to bear on the committee which had already got to work on the revision of the Book of Common Prayer.[1] His interest in revision had been aroused when he had to conduct impromptu services for the troops on the Nile in 1916 and, after the War, for the highly critical students at Knutsford. Although he had a great reverence for the language of Cranmer, he was convinced that revision was long overdue. The book which this group produced in 1923, and became known as 'the Grey Book' on account of the colour of its cover, shows the mark of Russell's hand throughout. The language of the Prayer Book is mainly retained: there is no suggestion of the substitution of 'you' for 'thou'. To that extent, the proposed revision seems very conservative today.

Russell was chiefly interested in the setting out of the lectionary in a more intelligible sequence and the omission of phrases which might be misleading to a generation that already was ceasing to read the Bible at home. Archaic expressions which had already aroused his ridicule, like 'followers of holy and godly matrons' were removed from the marriage service, as

[1] The Bishops produced their proposals in 1927. These were accepted by the Church Assembly but twice rejected by Parliament in 1927-8. In spite of this rejection the 1928 Book has been much used in parish churches ever since. The Grey Book is largely forgotten but it had some influence on the official revisers.

was the word 'obey' from the bridal promise. The most radical change in the book was in the baptismal rite. Russell and his friends were well aware that more non-churchgoers attended for church baptisms, weddings, and funerals, than at any other time. To make the service intelligible, even to the most theologically illiterate, they dropped the traditional 'born in sin' and substituted for it the rather banal statement with which none could disagree, 'It is plain that human nature as we see it ourselves and in the whole race of mankind is not what God our father intends it to be.' This passage reflects the characteristic Pelagianism of English theology in the post-war years which is not entirely absent from the 1928 book.[1] Later on Russell came to revise his views about this tendency in Anglican theology.

Just before leaving Knutsford, Russell had taken part in the 1923 Mission to Cambridge University, speaking for six nights in succession at Holy Trinity Church where Edward Woods was vicar. He decided to direct his challenge more to the mind than to the emotions. After his first address, the vicar turned to Russell in the vestry and told him that his approach was far too highbrow and that he must take a simpler line. Russell rejected this advice, and rightly so, because only a few years later he was to fill St. Mary's, Oxford, to capacity with a similar style of preaching.

At the outset of his career a young theologian has to make a choice which will determine his future work. Either he must devote his time exclusively to research within a university and produce now and then a learned book, 'more and more about less and less', or else he must decide to harness his scholarship to the propagation of a particular point of view in the church at large. Russell made his choice in 1919 when he resigned his fellowship at Oriel and accepted the offer of Knutsford. He became a passionate propagandist of applied liberal theology. He was a master of language and had a nimble wit, a combination of assets which render their possessor vulnerable to certain temptations. He was criticized in the *Church Times* by a reviewer for 'writing with more of the fervour of an advocate than the impartiality of a judge'. Later Dr. Pickard Cambridge, a colleague at Oxford, shot at him the kind of quip in which dons delight to indulge at the expense of their fellows: 'Barry will always lack the precision of a scholar while he is so perfectly at the mercy of an effective turn of phrase'. A similar criticism was made of the youthful William Temple: 'he thinks he has found a solution when he has only found a phrase.' But Russell had definitely turned aside from the path of pure scholarship when he accepted Knutsford and in his defence it might be argued that anyone who thinks he has something important to say and wants the maximum number of people to listen is bound to admit bias into his pronouncements. Literature without bias would be almost unreadable, as Professor G. M. Trevelyan was at pains to point out. But Russell's reading was so wide, his memory so retentive, and his intelligence so sharp, that generally his subjective judgments were well informed and under scholarly restraint.

When the offer came to Russell he felt himself unqualified for the Professorship at King's. Considering he had spent three years in the army and

---

[1] In place of the words 'born in sin' in the baptismal service, the words 'prone to sin' were substituted in the 1928 Book.

another three at Knutsford teaching and guiding young men whose education in some cases was limited and in all cases interrupted by the war, this is not surprising. Nevertheless had he chosen a purely academic career he would soon have made himself adequate to teach post-graduate students at any level. But the vocation to propagate his convictions as widely as possible within the Church and beyond and to relate the Christian faith to actual situations turned him away from pure academic research. It was on a walk with Mervyn Haigh on the Lulworth Downs that it came home to him that the Christian ethic, 'cannot be derived simply from direct quotations from the Gospels or applying the Sermon on the Mount but that the actual content of the Christian life must always be variable and contextual.' It is not surprising that the more venturesome of his students found Russell's views on ethics refreshing and challenging, but that others who vainly imagined that every ethical problem can be resolved by resort to a text in the Gospels, were alarmed.

It was at King's that Russell's theology matured and took shape in a mould which was to characterize his prophetic utterances till the end of his life. He had, as he admitted in his autobiography, an old-fashioned personal religion which he inherited from his home and from the nineteenth century Anglicanism in which he was reared. It was this that prevented him from going over whole-heartedly to the Modern Churchman's Union and differentiated his approach to theology from that of Bishop Barnes. On the other hand, Russell, like many modernists, had been given by nature an enquiring and sceptical mind. At King's he acquired a nice, if sometimes uneasy, balance between the two strains in his make-up. He appreciated the point of Sir Edwyn Hoskyns' complaint, 'Oh those accursed theologians who instead of being on their knees before the Cross are sitting on the throne of God asking him questions!' and the dry comment of the high church vicar in Leeds to his curate after they had been summoned by the Bishop of Ripon to a synod in Harrogate on the theme 'The Rediscovery of God': 'I always thought it was man that was lost but now I am told it is God, and we are bidden by the Bishop to find him in Harrogate.' Yet Russell gave the title *Asking the Right Questions* to one of his last books and he was asking questions of traditional theology till within a few days of his death. This poem appeared in a church newspaper over Russell's initials after a meeting of the Modern Churchman's Union at Somerville College, Oxford, in 1924:

All Things New

(Dedicated to all modern Churchmen with a sense of humour)

> Modern churchmen are sure that Psychology
> Has left us without a theology:
> But the sinner can still be redeemed if he will
> take a First Class degree in Biology.
>
> Though the highbrows grow daily more tall in it
> (for there's very small risk of a fall in it)
> Yet Elijah and Moses (knowing naught of neuroses)
> are shut out and you won't find St. Paul in it.

The multitude no man can number
The tinker and tailor and plumber
and the 'Wayfaring Man'
must read Barnes if it can
and if not there is no room for such lumber.

So the songs of the Saints will grow sager
but as for the simple, I wager,
though faith, hope and love may be mentioned above
Yet greater will also be Major.

                                          F.R.B.

In 1926 the offer of St. Mary the Great, the University Church of Cambridge, came from Trinity College. It was here that the University sermons were preached but the pulpit had ceased to attract either undergraduates in the mornings or townsfolk in the evenings. He turned to B. K. Cunningham and Edward Woods for advice. Both strongly urged him not to accept on the grounds that St. Mary's was a dead horse which no amount of beating could revive. For the second time Edward Woods' advice was to be proved by the turn of events to have been wrong. If Russell had accepted St. Mary's in 1926, he would have done for Cambridge what he was to do for Oxford two years later when he accepted the University church there. As it was, St. Mary's, Cambridge, had to wait nearly thirty years for a revival which Russell could have anticipated in the nineteen twenties.

A year later came offers of St. Mary, Portsea, and St. Mary the Virgin, Oxford. Portsea had at that time a tremendous reputation. Lang and Garbett had both been vicar there and it was generally regarded as a stepping stone to a diocese. It served a great working-class parish in the heart of Portsmouth. Next to the vicarage was a clergy house accommodating twelve stalwart curates, all of them graduates of one of the two ancient universities. Once again princes of the church fought over Russell's body. Garbett, now Bishop of Southwark and a close friend of Russell's, urged him to accept Portsea. The Archbishops of Canterbury and York, Davidson and Lang, pressed the claims of St. Mary, Oxford. Portsea could not be lightly turned down. It had a large congregation, a more than adequate staff, a benefice house and an income, as well as a great reputation. St. Mary's had great traditions but they were largely buried in its past. It had practically no congregation and the warnings of Edward Woods and B. K. Cunningham about St. Mary's, Cambridge, applied equally to it. There was no benefice house and practically no income. Russell with considerable courage and faith accepted it. Had he been a married man with a family he would have been in no position to do so. But it would have been disastrous for him had he gone to Portsea. He was brilliant at giving younger men a vision and a challenge in their student days, but he would not have been suitable either by temperament or experience to supervise the activities of a team of curates engaged in house-to-house visiting, Sunday schools, and boys' clubs. The vital decision he made in 1927 was the right one for him and for the Church.

5. NEWMAN'S PULPIT—ANOTHER VOICE

I

Once he had accepted St. Mary's, Russell was faced with what appeared to be an insoluble financial problem. The endowment income of the benefice amounted to about £130 per annum and in those days there was no scheme of diocesan augmentation. St. Mary's was in the gift of Oriel, and his predecessor had held a fellowship there which provided him with an extra income as well as accommodation in the college. But tension between him and the fellows made them reluctant to take the new vicar into their midst. So the fellowship which Russell had relinquished at the end of the war was not offered back to him.

It was Balliol who came to the rescue. A. D. Lindsay, the Master, was on the lookout for an assistant chaplain because the official chaplain, a fellow of the college and a distinguished lecturer in English, did not conceal his distaste for pastoral work and had made it clear that he would welcome neither confidences nor requests for spiritual counsel. Russell, whose reputation as a pastor amongst students had come ahead of him to Oxford, was the obvious person to fill the vacuum caused by the chaplain's short-comings. In return for a small stipend and rooms in college he was invited to give some tutorials in philosophy, preach occasionally in the college chapel, and keep a pastoral eye on the students. The appointment gave him a status in the University but it also involved him in extra work. On his own admission, his Plato and Aristotle had become rather rusty and needed some polishing up before he was able to give tutorials in philosophy.

The Oxford to which Russell returned in 1927 had changed considerably since 1915 but in retrospect it can now be seen that in spite of the upheaval of war and its aftermath, the University still belonged more to its past than to its future. The tone was still set by the public schools. The majority of the undergraduates came from middle-class homes, their fees paid by their fathers. Sport still attracted much attention in the life of the colleges. Women had now become full members of the University but played a comparatively small part in its social life. The men were still conditioned to a largely masculine existence.

Most of the young men were up for a good time, rejoicing in their emancipation from school discipline which had included compulsory attendance at chapel. A lot of beer was drunk and noise made on festive occasions but all that added up to little more than what Gibbon described indulgently as, 'the brisk intemperance of youth'. But however lightheartedly the under-graduates took their privileged years at Oxford, the Empire still loomed large in the 1920s and it was for some sort of service in the Empire that many of the ablest among them were destined. Jowett's ideal of a university provid-ing education for servants of the state still lingered on and ambitious young men who shared it had to take their work seriously. A place in the Sudan Civil Service was reputed to require a First in the Schools and a Blue, and achievement in either sphere demanded a considerable degree of self-imposed discipline.

Although most of the undergraduates did not, on the surface, appear to be unduly concerned, it was quite clear in 1927 that the course of world events was not going according to the optimistic expectations of 1919. Dr. Homes Dudden, the Head of an Oxford College, preaching a university sermon at Cambridge in 1931, probably voiced the inner feelings of many of the young men at Oxford when he said, 'We have been woefully let down. Our hopes have not been realized.' But when, five years before, the General Strike had broken out, many undergraduates took it as an opportunity for a lark. Their manning of trains and buses indicated no political bias against the strikers. The political temperature of the University remained fairly low while Russell was at St. Mary's compared with what it was to become in the late thirties after he had moved on to Westminster. Pacifism did not become a live issue until the menace of Hitler began to disturb the peace of Europe after 1933 and it was the Spanish Civil War which broke out in 1936 that really did raise the political heat in the universities, forcing young men and women to make a choice between Right and Left.

The majority of undergraduates in 1927 coming from the public schools were accustomed to regular church attendance and were familiar with *Hymns Ancient and Modern* and the Book of Common Prayer. They had listened or gone through the motions of listening to seventy-two sermons from the chapel pulpit during the school year and most of them had been confirmed as a matter of course. But there was a feeling that much that had been put across by way of religious instruction at home and at school was open to question. A general spirit of cynical indifference to institutional religion prevailed. Chapel was no longer compulsory as it had been in Russell's days.

As soon as an undergraduate arrived at Oxford he was made aware of a wide variety of religious societies claiming his allegiance. The S.C.M. had a fairly numerous following but in the years since the war had lost much of its thrust. It seemed to be more concerned about what Christianity wasn't than what it was. The O.I.C.C.U. was the most clamorous of all the religious societies and had a committed representative in every college. It was hearty, philistine, narrowly dogmatic in tone. Although it boasted many converts from the ranks of the freshmen, in fact its membership really depended on men who had already been converted as schoolboys in Crusader classes, Inter-varsity and Public School camps, and evangelical churches up and down the country. A young man who stayed within this society throughout his university career could only do so by keeping his faith in a water-tight compartment, well away from any radical thinking. The discipline of the Society virtually robbed him of the opportunity of making any friends outside the O.I.C.C.U. and of taking from the university much that it had to offer. It must, however be admitted that many men who owed their faith to the O.I.C.C.U. and later struck out roots in a more liberal soil benefitted from the deep grounding in religion they had been given in their impressionable years. Others reacted violently from the incredible fundamentalism upon which the O.I.C.C.U. insisted.

Apart from the S.C.M. and the O.I.C.C.U. with their large membership, there was the numerically smaller and rather exotic group of high church undergraduates who centred on Pusey House. With all the cocksureness of youth, they assumed that in their liturgical and devotional practice and discipline, they alone did things correctly. There were scholars amongst them to support them in their views but their influence was limited. Equally exclusive was the group of Roman Catholics gathered around Ronald Knox at the Old Palace in St. Aldate's. Converts in the years after the war included a number of celebrities, like Christopher Hollis, son of an Anglican bishop, whose friends at that time predicted for him a brilliant political career, and Evelyn Waugh. Their conversion caused a mild sensation in university and Church circles. Ronald Knox, who had debated with Russell at Oriel before the war when he was still an Anglican, had been described, not with exaggeration, as the wittiest young man in England. He was a much sought-after speaker at every kind of society, including the Union. His books were widely read, but as a religious leader he made little impact except on a rather exclusive coterie of 'upper crust' catholics who laughed at his jokes and revelled in his society. No ex-grammar school boy would have been at home in their company. Knox was clearly contemptuous of the science faculties in the University, and deliberately remained ignorant of their activities. He belonged to an Oxford (and indeed to a world) which was already vanishing and for many of his friends that was one of his attractions.

On to the comparative calm of University life there burst in the twenties a quasi-religious movement which caused something of a stir, not on account of any intrinsic merit in its doctrines, for it had no doctrines, but because it succeeded in winning over temporarily several prominent senior members of the University as well as some notable athletes amongst the under-graduates, of a type who previously would have been regarded as proof against any form of religious commitment. The so-called 'Oxford Group' had an uncanny knack of touching on the exposed nerves of uneasy consciences, thereby causing sharp reactions. Its adherents claimed that by waiting upon the guidance of the Holy Spirit every day they could achieve absolute standards of purity and honesty. These claims, when not examined too closely, made an instant appeal and many dramatic 'changes' were recorded and loudly advertised. But when on closer inspection it was discovered that infallibility in guidance, such as the Pope himself might envy, inevitably fell to the strongest-minded member present and that many leaders of the Group fell below the absolute standards they proclaimed, reaction set in and the last state of the convert was often worse than the first. Oxford greatly needed wise counsellors to pick up the casualties.

The Oxford of 1927 though reacting from Victorian ethics and sceptical of traditional Christian dogma had not yet completely broken with its religious past. Philosophy was still taught by teachers in the old tradition. A young man reading Greats might well feel the tension between the philosopher's unfettered search for truth and the revealed religion of the theologian. But philosophers and theologians were breathing in the same metaphysical atmosphere. They were still on speaking terms. Hence the success of Temple's Mission in 1931. It was not until 1936, three years after Russell had left Oxford, that A. J. Ayer, then a research student of Christ Church, dropped his bomb-shell on the University by the publication of his book,

Language, Truth and Logic, which insisted that any form of metaphysical statement, let alone Christian dogma, was meaningless. Nothing could be sensibly stated that was not open to verification which, according to Ayer, meant the verification of the laboratory. After that not only in Oxford but widely amongst the new generation, as Russell was to complain, metaphysics became a 'dirty word' for people who had neither heard of Ayer nor read his book. But all this lay in the future when Russell came back to Oxford in 1927. When Russell left St. Mary's, the book which caused the explosion was still in manuscript form in a young man's room in Christ Church, and a Master of Balliol was still concerned that a Christian pastorate should be brought to bear on the young men in his college.

II

Russell's impact on Balliol was immediate. Undergraduates were soon coming to consult him about every subject under the sun, or so it seemed to them. On Sunday nights his rooms were packed to capacity until the small hours of Monday morning. He gave tutorials in philosophy and preached in the college chapel when his duties at St. Mary's allowed. One of his Balliol pupils writes, 'We found him a prophet and more than a prophet, a delicious human counsellor who would talk on anything and whose simian features lit up with loving amusement.' The quips which came off his tongue like darts from a blow-pipe are still remembered fifty years later. To an undergraduate who came for advice about living more simply, he replied, 'The trouble about living a simple life is that it is so frightfully expensive.' A young man with doubts which hitherto he had kept to himself, certainly from the school chaplain and the vicar, was reassured when told, 'The man who says he never had any doubts can be a saint. He is much more likely to be a perfect fool.' At that time Gilbert Murray was proclaiming himself an unbeliever. Russell surprised a smoke-filled room of undergraduates by commenting, 'I do wish Gilbert Murray would stop this nonsense of saying he is an atheist. I want to ask him to preach at St. Mary's.' He had already acquired many of the mannerisms in speech and gesture which were to be accentuated in old age. At a Swanwick Conference one of his pupils who was an excellent mimic, gave a very good imitation of the vicar of St. Mary's in the pulpit. 'Who is this viper I have nursed in my bosom?' commented Russell, highly amused.

Russell was very much sought after by undergraduates for advice on their future careers. Later he was to write books about vocation to the ministry and was to be a chairman of the C.A.C.T.M. Committee involved in recruitment. He always watched for the right sort of men for ordination. Quite a number came up to Oxford with ordination in mind, wavered in their vocation, and were helped back to it by him. After a few moments' talk it became plain that it was still possible to combine intellectual integrity with Christian belief. But one of his students remembers gratefully that Russell warned him off ordination and advised him to be a schoolmaster instead. After fifty years this man is convinced that the advice was sound. 'I was so much under his spell at that time that I would have done anything he told me to do.' Many men who later rose to the top of their professions are still grateful to Russell for putting their feet on the first step of the ladder to a distinguished and useful career.

Soon after he arrived at Oxford, Russell was faced with a situation which was both embarrassing and painful. Leonard Wilson, who later was to become Bishop of Singapore and eventually of Birmingham, had been one of his most promising pupils at Knutsford and remained a close friend to the end of his life. It was his habit to consult Russell before making any important decision. In 1927 he was accepted by the Church Missionary Society for work in Cairo and thus came under the jurisdiction of Bishop Gwynne, Russell's old chief in France. Wilson at thirty was still a rather complex character. His schooldays at St. John's, Leatherhead, had been very unhappy. He had got into the army just before the end of the war by giving a false age. When the war came to an end he volunteered for ordination, confiding to a friend that it was his intention not to be like other parsons. He was naturally rebellious and this partly accounts for his unhappiness at school and for many awkward incidents in the course of his life. He was an advanced modernist; in fact just the kind of young man whom Russell delighted to handle. Knutsford under Barry with his sympathy for restless and questing youth was exactly the right training-ground for him.

When Wilson arrived in Cairo he found that the post to which he had been appointed had not yet fallen vacant and so was left kicking his heels for several months. He was an extremely sociable person with a gift for getting on with people, in particular with the sort of English people who had little in common with the average C.M.S. missionary. He was invited to preach several times in the Cathedral where his sermons were appreciated by those members of the congregation who were not averse to having their minds stretched. These same sermons were not so acceptable to conservative evangelicals of whom there were a number in Cairo at that time in close touch with the C.M.S.

Wilson did not believe that the salvation of mankind depended on the historicity of the Virgin Birth and this heterodox point of view became evident in one of his sermons, which he doubtless preached all the more confidently because he knew the theology behind it was shared by his revered chief at Knutsford. There were of course members of the C.M.S. who sympathized with a liberal approach to Christian dogma, but the Society, though not fundamentalist, still tended to be conservative in its theology. Wilson had not learned the lesson which many others have had to learn that although doctrinal liberalism is tolerated in the Church of England and, in fact, has an honourable tradition within it, membership of certain church societies requires discretion in admitting to it. Russell himself had to learn this lesson in his dealing with the Mothers' Union. Bishop Gwynne was a loving, sympathetic and wise pastor, but on this occasion it would appear that his sympathies could not be stretched to embrace a rather conceited young man with advanced modernistic views who seemed to enjoy causing feathers to fly in respectable C.M.S. circles in his diocese. He decided to abandon Wilson. More than that, he refused to grant him a personal interview. As a result, Wilson wrote the bishop what one can only hope was the rudest letter he ever wrote to anyone in the course of his life.

In the summer of 1928 both the bishop and Wilson were in England. Wilson made straight to Oxford to consult Russell who found himself poised between his beloved chief of army days and one of his favourite Knutsford pupils. It was an embarrassing and painful situation. The advice he gave is printed in full in Roy McKay's *Life of Leonard Wilson.* It reveals very clearly the breadth of Russell's theological thinking at that time . . .

'I would say quite definitely if you are forced to resign on these grounds [his liberal approach to the Virgin Birth] the C.M.S. will make it quite impossible for a moderate liberal to support them. It is not a question of what is called Modernism but of such elementary recognition of the great issues raised in theology as ought to be required as a condition of ordination from any candidate for the ministry.'

Encouraged by Russell, Wilson resigned from the C.M.S. and returned to County Durham as a curate. Bishop Gwynne cancelled a visit to Oxford which he had promised Russell and returned to Egypt. Considering his reputation as a pastor, his conduct in this unfortunate episode is inexplicable. Unfortunately any papers that Russell may have kept were destroyed in the Blitz.

III

It was, of course, to St. Mary's and not to Balliol that Russell was brought back to Oxford in the first place. Although it was the University Church and in it the statutory sermons had always been preached, it had a small parish. This consisted chiefly of college quadrangles, which did not come under the vicar's jurisdiction in any case, and part of the High Street. The resident parishioners were described by Russell rather naughtily as 'all druggists and chemists'. It was not to them that he mainly addressed himself. His aim was to make St. Mary's the church of the University in fact as well as in name.

From the moment Russell appeared in the pulpit which Newman had occupied a century before, congregations began to grow and within a few months the church was so full that he sometimes had difficulty in reaching the steps. Most of the congregation were students but a number of dons and their families walked in from North Oxford on Sunday mornings. These included the formidable Mrs. Creighton, widow of the Bishop, whose daughter was married to a fellow of Balliol. It was she who told Russell when he visited her on a bed of sickness that he didn't know his job. The undergraduates seemed to have thought otherwise. A former member of his congregation remembers hurrying through dinner in hall in order to secure a seat in the church for the eight o'clock service which Russell introduced. 'He provided us with strong meat and plenty of food for thought. His preaching was dynamic, electrifying.' He did much of the preaching himself and in the opinion of many members of the congregation his sermons were more effective than those preached by distinguished visitors from outside. At this time an invitation to the pulpit at St. Mary's was regarded as a compliment and some who fancied themselves qualified for it were offended when none arrived. Bishop Winnington-Ingram, who in his heyday had filled St. Mary's and had enthralled Russell as an undergraduate, made it quite clear that he expected to be invited. But, by 1930, the old man had preached himself out; his sermons were mere repetitions of those he had preached before the war and were trenchantly described by Russell himself as pathetic. They had, of course, crossed swords in 1915. Russell relented with reluctance and many misgivings and invited the bishop to preach, only to be told before the service began that the vestry must be left open for him at the end because a large number of young men would be flooding in to consult the preacher. 'Thank goodness,' remarked Russell rather unkindly with a flick of his tongue, 'only one came.'

As we have seen, when Russell came to Oxford the S.C.M. was in low water. He helped to revive it and before he left it had become a very effective Christian movement in the University, attracting many men and women of ability into its ranks. Russell was a frequent speaker at its meetings both in Oxford and at the conference house at Swanwick in Derbyshire. He acted as a kind of senior friend and advisor and on several occasions was consulted by the Executive Committee about appointments He was greatly helped in this particular field by Harry Baynes, his curate at St. Mary's, who previously had been an S.C.M. secretary in London.

When Russell became a bishop it was noticeable that he was reluctant to take part in money-raising activities, however much he was in sympathy with the object for which an appeal had been made. The diocese would have been surprised had it known that during his vicariate at St. Mary's in the years before the war, he had made quite a name for himself as a money-raiser and had experienced all the trials and tribulations involved in putting through an imaginative plan of church restoration. In 1927 the interior of St. Mary's remained more or less as it was when Newman left it three quarters of a century before. The prestige of a church may be increased by having a great historic name associated with it but there are disadvantages, one of which is that part of itself is buried in the past. Many people, particularly those who do not have to worship in it regularly, are convinced that any change in the fabric or furnishing amounts to a slight on the memory of the great man.

Newman had filled the church with a large congregation as, in fact, Russell was to do himself a century later. The congregation overflowed into a hideous gallery which completely covered the north aisle and even protruded into the nave itself, thus robbing a fine mediaeval church of its graceful proportions. Russell's plans for the removal of the gallery had considerable support from members of the congregation, but there was some hot opposition from senior members of the University including Sir Michael Sadler, the Master of University College down the High Street. Russell persevered with his intentions and finally succeeded in converting Sir Michael into a warm supporter of the scheme which was brought to a triumphant conclusion shortly before he left. 'I gave the University back its church' was his proud boast. He gave the University much else beside.

The highlight of Russell's ministry at St. Mary's was William Temple's Mission to the University in 1931. Russell was largely responsible for the arrangements and also for entertaining the missioner. For seven nights in succession the Archbishop preached in St. Mary's to a packed church. A very high proportion of the undergraduate population heard him on at least one occasion. Many went every night and admitted later on that Temple's presentation of the Christian faith made a permanent impression on their lives. Russell himself was to comment that there was a lot of cynicism and scepticism at the time and Temple's Mission 'stopped the rot.'

Looking back after forty years it might be more accurate to say that the Mission rekindled the smouldering embers of Christianity in a University which in 1931 could still be described loosely as Christian but which was so soon to cease to be Christian except in name. Pockets of Christianity, of course, remain to this day. But at least this much can be said for Russell's ministry at St. Mary's: it enabled large numbers of young men in the 1920s and '30s to go out into positions of responsibility in peace and war with a faith which would have wavered and perhaps evaporated had it not been for the preaching of F. R. Barry. Of course there were other Oxfords during this period which were not touched by the ministry at St. Mary's. The Oxford of Maurice Bowra, of Evelyn Waugh and, in the last years before the Second World War, of Richard Hilary passed it by. The men who came under Russell's influence were of a serious turn of mind, expecting to serve the Empire in one capacity or another, to teach in the Public Schools, or to become clergy in the Anglican Church at home and overseas—professional men in responsible positions. Many of them were to serve in the war.

IV

In 1929 to the surprise of his friends who regarded him as a confirmed bachelor, Russell got married. Lilian Gray was the daughter of Buchanan Gray, Professor of Old Testament at Mansfield, a Congregational college in Oxford. She went to Girton College, Cambridge, and returned to Oxford to look after her mother on her father's death and to become secretary to the historian, H. A. L. Fisher. Whilst with him she typed out the whole of his great work, *The History of Europe*. Russell also wanted secretarial assistance while he was writing *The Relevance of Christianity*, and Lilian came to his rooms at Balliol to do the typing. It was she who suggested the title for the book. As he puts it in his autobiography, 'I was in a very vulnerable position.' They got engaged on the Berkshire Downs above Wantage and were married by Russell's father, assisted by Cyril Garbett, with Mervyn Haigh as best man, at the University Church which was packed for the occasion. Marriage made it necessary for the Barrys to look for a vicarage, and a small house was found in Holywell. A graduate of Cambridge herself, Lilian had lived all her early life in Oxford and therefore fully understood university life. Her presence in a home of their own domesticated Russell's hospitality. His deafness was already becoming more marked and his need for assistance in entertaining was all the greater.

6. THORNEY ISLAND

I

When Russell went to St. Mary's, Oxford, in 1927 the storm clouds had not yet gathered over Europe. It is true that Mussolini had taken charge in Italy, and people of perception were aware that his coup was a setback to democracy and peace. But many British holiday-makers excused the Fascist regime on the grounds that Italy was Italy and that trains now ran to time and their luggage was not so likely to be stolen from the guard's van. It was not generally believed that world peace was threatened and there was an underlying assumption that Europeans would never be so mad as to resort to war again.

When Russell moved to Westminster in 1933 the international scene had changed. Hitler had just established himself in Germany and the possibility of a future war again had to be reckoned with. Pacifism was becoming a lively issue. Fifty years afterwards it is difficult to recall the shock that the prospect of a renewal of hostilities inflicted on those ex-servicemen whose morale had been buoyed up in the trenches by the assurance that at least they were giving their lives and limbs in a war to end war. Talk of rearmament seemed like a betrayal of dead comrades. For liberals it was also a betrayal of that tradition in which they had been reared and which had now become a part of their being, a tradition which was inspired by Christian hope blended uncomfortably with a pseudo-Darwinian evolutionary philosophy. For those who represented this tradition, the Great War had been seen more as a setback to their optimism than as the destruction of it. Now Russell and many like him were becoming painfully aware that it might be more than a setback.

The prospect of war dominated his message in the pulpit for the next eight years. He had been, as a young man, a prophet of crisis, and he began to return to that role again at Westminster. Yet in his autobiography he had to admit that these were happy days. He had a job after his own heart and an audience such as he delighted to address. No. 2 Little Cloisters, one of the finest houses in London, was the loveliest in which he and his wife were ever to live. They were now the proud possessors of a baby daughter. They had an adequate domestic staff. Above all, for Russell the Abbey symbolized all that he admired most in the Church-State connection. He loved to show his friends round the royal tombs at night by torchlight, a quite unforgettable experience. It meant much to him that as a canon he had to carry the Bible at the Coronation of King George VI and took part in other great ceremonial services of national significance. Although he was impatient of ritualism of a purely ecclesiastical kind, he relished to the full ceremonies which blended national, historical and ecclesiastical ingredients. He looked to the Church to enrich and sanctify the State, and the State on occasions to correct the vagaries of ecclesiastics where they affected adversely the body politic.

Once again Russell found himself with a double job. He had his residence and duties at the Abbey. He was also Rector of St. John's, Smith Square, a few hundred yards away, which not only had an eclectic congregation drawn from all over the metropolis, but a densely populated working-class area in the immediate vicinity. There was a dichotomy at the heart of the parish, with its dignified Queen Anne houses around the church where many members of both Houses of Parliament lived and, at the other end of Great Peter Street, the blocks of tenement houses to which people had been moved after the flooding of the Thames embankment in 1928.

Russell's predecessor, C. S. Woodward, who had just gone on to be Bishop of Bristol, had kept both elements of the population in hand but not in the same hand. Before he went to Westminster, he had been vicar of a fashionable West End parish where he had introduced a very popular service for children which had been taken up by the B.B.C. and frequently broadcast. Many of the children came to these services accompanied by their nannies. At St. John's Woodward introduced the same sort of service, but he was also immensely popular with the children from the tenement houses. He used to read books to them sitting on the bottom step of the communal staircases. When his tall, gaunt figure was spotted in the street the cry of 'the Rector' would go up and in a moment, like the children of Hamelin at the sound of the piper's pipe, a hoard of youngsters would come rushing down the staircases, to leap all over him clinging to his arms and climbing over his shoulders.

Russell could not attempt to maintain this type of popularity. His gifts were very different from Woodward's. He had loved 'Tommy' in Egypt and in Flanders and had got on well with him, but he was not adept at house-to-house visiting and the small talk involved in it. So, when the children way-laid him in the street as they had done his predecessor, he found their attentions embarrassing. He was always allergic to the tactile approach, whether in the form of an overhearty handshake or a pat on the back. At St. John's he left the ministry of the tenements largely to a succession of able young curates and concentrated on those parishioners with whom he had intellectual affinities. It was the most sensible and profitable course for him to take. There were then, as now, very few clergy, even in the highest echelons of the Church, more capable than Russell of commending the Christian faith to intelligent and educated enquirers.

The curates carried on without much supervision from the rector. As at Southwell later on, his calling of staff meetings was spasmodic. When the staff did get together he always hoped for evidence of success to reassure him that the Church really was getting to grips with the working classes. In fact the curates did good work amongst the young people in the tenement houses, but Russell sometimes appeared not to be altogether impressed with it. They on their part complained that when they did succeed in persuading some of the young people to come to St. John's for evensong, the Rector preached over their heads. Russell had always been given to quips about the strange ways of ecclesiastics: but now a rather cynical note crept into his conversation. Once at a staff meeting when they were discussing some parochial project, he blurted out, 'If this fails we shall have shot our bolt.' Those who knew him well made allowances, but newcomers to his staff could be startled and discouraged. It seemed to at least one of his curates that he was too much absorbed with success.

Russell had from his youth been on easy terms with many of the ecclesiastical hierarchy from Lambeth downwards. At Oxford he mixed freely with distinguished academics. At Westminster he began to meet people who were playing an important part in the life of the nation, and his ambition that the Church should be 'put on the map' was heightened. It was noticed by some of his friends that his own place in the career structure of the Church was not altogether absent from his mind. Years later in his autobiography he was to confess that if the Church were true to itself, it should not be concerned with worldly success. In 1938 he would have had difficulty in convincing some of those who knew and admired him that he really believed that.

The congregation at St. John's could hardly be described as parochial. Although a number of parishioners attended, the majority were educated people from all over London who were attracted by Russell's style of preaching. After it had been announced in the Press on Saturday morning that the Rector was preaching the following day there was a packed church, but when it was the turn of one of the curates, the congregation was very thin. Russell was so concerned at the lack of fellowship in the congregation that he started a weekly luncheon club at Caxton Hall at which he always gave a brief talk before the company dispersed.

One of Russell's most successful achievements as Rector of St. John's was the launching of the parish magazine in a new form in January 1941 during the aerial bombardment of Westminster and at one of the darkest periods of the war. He called it *The Thorney Island Review,* explaining in the first editorial that the Palace of Westminster had risen in a reedy swamp half in and half out of the River Thames, which the Benedictine monks cleared in the eleventh century for the building of their monastery. It suited Russell's broad perspective of the ups and downs of history that the Mother of Parliaments should have grown up in what had been originally such an unpropitious site. As was to be expected, the *Review* from the beginning was more than a parish magazine. Russell refused to include parochial chitchat and concentrated on articles of the same quality as were to appear in the *Southwell Review* a few years later on. The *Thorney Island Review* was read far beyond the boundaries of the parish and brought a message of faith and hope to a beleaguered country in one of the most gloomy periods of the war.

Russell visited the sick assiduously. He was appointed chaplain of the Greycoat School for Girls where he took confirmation classes for a group of sixth formers who had escaped the net of confirmation in their home parishes. Over these classes he took a great deal of trouble. One of his confirmation candidates at the Greycoat School after forty years remembers his 'shy half-smile' as he passed the girls in the corridors, the seriousness with which he listened to their questions in class and the amount of mental effort he put into the answering of them. The girls were as much impressed by his complete lack of pomposity as they were by his erudition. He never talked down to them and to their surprise he seemed to know a lot more about young people than they had ever imagined a dignitary of the Church would do. He was very different from their fathers and indeed from any other man they had ever met. They heard he had a little daughter of his own called Rosemary. They wondered what it would be like to be his child. It was a pity they never had an opportunity of seeing him tobogganing with Rosemary in the Christmas holidays.

Echoes of a conversation between Russell and a young couple who had asked him to marry them float down the years. The young lady had been a member of his congregation at St. Mary's, Oxford, where she had found his preaching like a 'gale of fresh air'. She could remember him reading his own banns and almost breaking down with embarrassment in the middle of them. Now she and her fiancé had come to put in their own. Russell sat them down and asked them if they wanted the 1662 or 1928 service. They had not previously given the matter any thought. After a pause, Russell said to the girl, 'Well, do you intend to obey Robert?' Again there was a pause before Russell broke in and said, 'Of course you don't, so don't start by saying you will.'[1] After that preliminary he went on to ask them if they wanted any kind of address and they thought that as he was a famous preacher he would almost certainly want to give one. But before they could give an answer he said, 'Well I won't. I should be very cross with anyone who wanted to preach at my wedding.' It is not surprising that after such bracing interviews many young couples who started married life in London flocked to Russell's house for further talks. One of those who went to these informal gatherings remembers him chuckling over the heresies which they propounded as if they were the first people ever to have thought of them. 'He would sit curled up in a big armchair chewing his pipe like a benign leprechaun.'

The headquarters of several national societies were housed in Great Peter Street. These included the Mary Sumner House. At that time Russell was critical of the Mothers' Union, perhaps not surprisingly considering it had recently banned one of his books which had contained a friendly reference to birth control. Showing a prospective curate round the parish, Russell, much to the surprise of the young man who was not accustomed to off-the-cuff quips by eminent divines, jerked his thumb in the direction of the building and said with a typical guffaw, 'That is the headquarters of the Mothers' Union. How I hate their morals!' Later as a bishop, he learnt to treat the Mothers' Union, as well as other societies with which he was not entirely in sympathy, with respect and consideration. In spite of his caustic and impish wit, he was essentially a gentle and kindly man.

As we have seen, Russell's preaching attracted people from all over London. In those days before the war the inhabitants of the West End still stayed in Town for the week-ends. The country cottage had not become the craze. As the clouds gathered over Europe, his preaching took on a more

---

[1] When twenty years later the author and his fiancée asked the bishop to marry them almost exactly the same conversation ensued. In this case they asked to include the word 'obey' and the bishop reluctantly agreed, but on the day the bishop left out the word and the bride, greatly daring but in a low voice, inserted it into her promise in spite of the bishop's omission.

and more sombre, even an apocalyptic, note. It seemed to one of his curates that in the pulpit he lost sight of the actual people below and was preaching out to the world—*urbi et orbi.* This was all right in the circumstances because the people who came to St. John's did so because they were looking for vision and prophecy. It was not so appropriate later when, as bishop, he preached in the village churches of Nottinghamshire. But his ministry in London did not end in words. After Munich when the Jewish victims of Hitler's persecution, some of them distinguished academics, artists and scientists, began to arrive in this country, Russell welcomed them in the name of St. John's and wherever possible found them accommodation and temporary work in London. Those who were Christian were brought right into the congregation, and on the eve of the war for several Sundays the Lord's Prayer was said in German as well as in English. This was the kind of pastoral work which appealed to Russell's imagination.

A tribute to Russell's ministry by one of the churchwardens at St. John's was included in the *Thorney Island Review* at the time of his departure to the Diocese of Southwell. It had been a daunting task to follow in the footsteps of Dr. C. S. Woodward who was described in this article as 'the greatest parish priest of his generation', but the author goes on to make it clear that the congregation which Russell inherited from Woodward and soon augmented by his own preaching was quick to realize that the people of St. John's were privileged to have a preacher and prophet of F. R. Barry's calibre and were proud that under his leadership the Church had become a spiritual power-house in the heart of London.

On the eve of Michaelmas 1938, at the height of the Munich crisis, Russell and a curate were walking through the Abbey cloisters. With the passage appointed for the epistle the following day in mind Russell said, 'There will be war in heaven tomorrow. Let us hope there won't be one on earth as well.' It was the same passage as had brought him light and refreshment after the Battle of the Somme in 1916. In the following months, when Hitler's deadly intentions were fully disclosed, and he heard first-hand accounts of the Nazi's treatment of the Jews, Russell abandoned the pacifist position to which he had become attracted in the early 1930s. His attitude towards pacifism had always been emotional rather than rational.

II

It would seem from the Chapter Minutes that Russell played a full part in the administration of the Abbey. Clergy with a national reputation already made, when preferred to cathedral chapters, have been known to disappear for weeks at a time and to re-surface only when the legal requirements of residence compel them to do so. Except when he was away in Australia and on one occasion when the Queen visited the Bluecoat School where he was a governor, Russell was exemplary in his attendance at Chapter. He was appointed successively Custodian, Steward, and then Librarian, with responsibility for the muniments and museum. He was present when they discussed the Abbey property, payment of cleaners and of vergers, the care of the gardens, and many other matters of a type which he tried to avoid when he became a diocesan bishop. It is not recorded if a debate on whether female visitors to the Abbey should be required to cover their heads evoked from him the comment, 'I don't suppose God cares much', which he was to make on other occasions when trivilities of this sort were heatedly argued by clergymen. He was no doubt more interested in a long discussion on whether Ramsay Macdonald's ashes should be offered burial in the Abbey. The Chapter was reluctant to create a precedent that every Prime Minister should have the privilege *ex officio*. In the event Macdonald's family resolved the question by expressing a preference for Lossiemouth as the place of burial for their father's remains.

Russell's most enduring contribution to the Abbey was his concern for air-raid precautions, once the possibility of another war was recognized as a probability. In 1938 he was made chairman of a sub-committee with authority to negotiate with the Westminster City Council. He arranged for the choirboys to be sent out of town during the Munich crisis. As Custodian he made plans for the Coronation Chair to be immured in the crypt of a provincial cathedral. In the event of invasion, Hitler was not to be afforded the satisfaction of sitting on the throne on which English sovereigns had been crowned since the time of Edward II.

In the early part of 1939 Russell carried through in the face of some local opposition plans for the building of an air-raid shelter in the Abbey garden, large enough to hold 160 people. It was objected that the unsightly concrete roof would spoil the appearance of the garden, which no doubt it did. It was completed in July 1939 just before the outbreak of war, and later was responsible for saving many lives.

III

When war broke out in September 1939, the congregation at St. John's began to disappear. 'Prophecy' as one of his former curates aptly put it, 'began to fade away not (as in the hymn) in the light of day but in the black-out.' When the bombing of London began in earnest the following year, Russell was out in the darkened streets every night visiting the distressed and the wounded in hospital, and helping to tend the casualties and to dig out bodies from the rubble. 'Well, we are saved,' he wrote in the *Thorney Island Review*, after a particularly bad spell of bombing, 'but so as by fire.'

Russell kept his head through it all, he even kept up his reading—presumably by taking a torch with him into the shelter at night. He had learnt twenty years before in France how to concentrate his attention on the pages of a book in the most unlikely situations. The *Review* included his comments on books which had engaged his attentions during these fearful months. After the destruction of St. John's, holy communion was celebrated in the chapel of S.P.G. House and carol services were held in the shelters at Christmas.

Throughout these troubled months at Westminster, Russell enjoyed a close friendship with the Dean, Paul de Labilliere. They were very different in scholarly attainment and habit of mind, but they each admired the other's qualities. Had he not had a vocation to holy orders, de Labilliere would almost certainly have gone into the army. He backed Russell's plans for air-raid precautions in 1938 and 1939 against all critics: and when the bombs began to fall they worked together in happy comradeship. Relations between members of the Abbey Chapter had not always been unanimously harmonious in the first half of this century. The relationship between Russell and de Labilliere could not have been happier.

Mr. T. Hebron who was then Registrar of the Abbey remembers Russell striding unconcerned through the Abbey garden with shrapnel and bomb splinters whistling through the trees, rushing into the blazing precincts one moment and then back to his stricken parish the next. He was, according to Mr. Hebron, an inspiration to them all. A similar tribute came from the churchwardens of St. John's. 'Utterly tireless, he worked continuously to improve conditions in the shelters and to inaugurate rest centres for the victims of the savagery of the enemy . . . he was incapable of thinking either of his own safety or of his own interests.' It was July 1916 all over again, with this difference: his home was just around the corner and his wife was by his side. Then on 10 May 1941 while he was keeping watch on the Abbey roof and putting out fire bombs which were raining on it, his house in the Little Cloisters with all its contents was destroyed. It was that night when he rang up 10 Downing Street and demanded special treatment for the Abbey which otherwise would have gone the way of his home.

Russell said later that it was a cathartic experience to be left with nothing but the clothes he stood up in, and these blackened with smoke. This was a brave boast. He was always a restless person and the loss of his home left him with a sense of rootlessness which was to prevent him easily settling into the new home which awaited him in the Midlands. For the months after the bombing of the Abbey and St. John's he had no home, no congregation, and no work to do. It came as a great relief when Winston Churchill's offer of the bishopric of Southwell arrived.

'FRB', Army Chaplain, 1919

'FRB', Canon of Westminster, 1937

7. SOUTHWELL

I

Like nearly all bishops, Russell had no briefing about his episcopal duties. In fact, as he tells us in his autobiography, Archbishop William Temple seemed rather surprised when he was asked at Bishopthorpe on the eve of the consecration for advice on one or two points of diocesan administration. If a new bishop had not come to the Bench by way of an archdeaconry or a suffragan bishopric it was unlikely that he knew much in advance about the duties that lay ahead of him. Unlike a deacon or a priest, a fledgling bishop entered upon a great responsibility without any coaching. Certainly, experience of St. Mary's Oxford and of a Canonry of Westminster provided very little by way of preparation for administering the diocese of Southwell. Russell was to confess to his chaplain after presiding over his first diocesan conference that it was the first time in his life that he had sat one through to the end. The poacher had become gamekeeper.

Russell had one idea of episcopal office firmly fixed in his mind until the day of his retirement. He had caught it from Randall Davidson. A bishop in the provinces of Canterbury and York should be more than a diocesan functionary. He regarded himself not only as bishop of a diocese, but also as a bishop of England. He would have deplored the modern habit of referring to bishops by their Christian name—'Bishop Brian' or 'Bishop Vyvian' instead of the 'Bishop of Barchester' with its territorial connotations. He never regarded the Church as a cosy little family isolated from the world. While he was Bishop of Southwell he was a frequent visitor to coal mines, factories, farms, schools and colleges and, above all, to the University of Nottingham.

Bishop Neville Talbot when welcoming the new bishop to the diocese said, 'The Bishop is in his own right a prophet. At York he has joined the glorious company of the apostles. It rests with us whether he is going to join the noble army of martyrs!' and then went on to warn the clergy not to call in the bishop every time something went wrong, as if he were the plumber. At that point Russell broke in, prophetically in view of his facility in the art of delegation, 'A plumber has a way of sending round his mate.'

As we have seen, Russell started at Southwell in the darkest days of the war when the energies of the whole population were absorbed in the struggle with Hitler and every kind of restriction was imposed on all activities which involved travel. Shortly after he arrived, he spoke wistfully of the silent belfries. If the church bells were heard again it would be as the sound of a tocsin. It was not until eleven months after his enthronement that they were rung again—gladly in celebration of the victory of Alamein.

Russell and Lilian were at first delighted with their new situation. He stood on the lawn in the sunshine and said 'Things don't happen like this in real life.' It was a great change from all the dust and rubble of London, and the welcome of the diocese was warm and encouraging. Friends rallied round to provide the empty house in Southwell with furniture. Some well-to-do laymen clubbed together to present the bishop with a cheque for the then substantial sum of £600. This was specially welcome to a family which had lost everything in the Blitz and before the days when the Commissioners covered the expenses of incoming bishops. Russell expressed his gratitude in no uncertain terms.

But somehow Southwell itself did not come up to expectations. Russell had lived in a village but never in a small provincial country town. The people of Southwell were kindly and expectant for they had all loved the Mosleys, but the town (it was never granted the status of a city even after its parish church had become a cathedral) was geriatric in character and its inhabitants inclined to the quiet life. If had no first-hand experience of the war, although sons of local residents were serving in the forces and some had already been killed or wounded. But after Oxford and Westminster the place seemed very unexciting. At this point Russell could have done with advice and encouragement from someone older and more experienced than himself. Shortly after his arrival, a guest at Bishop's Manor left a light on in the spare room after the black-out and the bishop was fined £2 in consequence. After his exploits in Westminster earlier that year he might have taken this ridiculous episode as a joke, but for once his sense of humour deserted him and he was very cross.

It is characteristic of the waywardness of human psychology that Russell needed the stimulus of an apocalyptic situation to bring the best out of him. The churchwarden of St. John's had noticed that no complaint had come from him when his house and all his belongings were devoured by the flames. Yet at Southwell he became increasingly addicted to grumbling about domestic irritations of trivial significance which he was apt to treat as major disasters. It was said of him that when high-explosive bombs were rained from the heavens he remained calm, but when a shower of rain came at an inconvenient moment, he treated it as a tragedy.

The house in which the Barrys had come to live had been built as a manor for the Archbishops of York in the Middle Ages. Wolsey is reputed to have stayed there after his disgrace. In the seventeenth century it had fallen into disrepair and only one wing had retained a roof over it and had become a farmhouse. In 1904 Bishop Hoskyns rebuilt the house within the ruins in such a way that Gothic windows and doorways appeared rather incongruously within a very twentieth century setting. The house had looked imposingly spacious when heavily furnished and pictured in Victorian style and there was a bevy of maids to look after it. It had a somewhat sepulchral air under wartime conditions.

II

Russell got out into the diocese immediately after his arrival. Winter was about to descend when the enthronement took place and he, who was never a competent motorist, had to find his way round an unknown countryside in the dark with dimmed headlights, often in the fog, and without the comforting guidance of 'cats-eyes' in the roads or even of signposts. Once in icy weather his car stopped and turned broadside on at the top of a hill bringing a convoy of lorries further down to a halt with little chance of starting up again. 'As you know,' he said to a vicar shortly afterwards, 'I have been through a world war and I have heard most things, but I think I heard more blasphemy that day in those three or four minutes.'[1] He was greatly helped in his early days by his chaplain, Noel Turner, vicar of Epperstone, who had been born and bred and served his whole ministry in Nottinghamshire. His local knowledge and friendship were of great assistance to the new bishop.

Russell insisted on taking all the institutions himself, thus identifying himself with a new incumbent from the outset, but he was very ill-at-ease in over-crowded schoolrooms and institutes where the party took place after the service. He might even have escaped from this embarrassment if if had not been for pressure put upon him by Archdeacon Hales. The deafening roar of conversation in a confined space accentuated his inability to hear what was said to him. It says all the more for his pastoral conscience that he insisted on doing the institutions himself and paying at least a token visit to the social gatherings afterwards, because at that time many bishops were still instituting new incumbents in their private chapels.

One other pastoral duty that Russell undertook from the beginning, which many contemporary bishops did not regard as a priority, was the regular visiting of the clergy in their homes. At first the appearance of the bishop emerging from his car without warning was an embarrassment to the clergy. They thought that the visit must have been occasioned by a complaint about their parochial behaviour. They were amazed to find that he had called for no other reason than that he wanted to get to know them in the context of their homes. His informal approach and complete lack of pomposity and his surprisingly unepiscopal asides soon put the clergy at their ease. He called up to a vicar in an apple-tree, 'Only wish I was so innocently employed.' To another vicar whom he found cleaning out a fireplace he said reassuringly, 'I am sure Bishop Andrewes would not have spent so long at his prayers if he had had to get down on his knees to clean the grates occasionally.' If he stayed for a meal he would sometimes insist on helping to wash up afterwards. On one occasion when he knocked at the front door the vicar's wife's head appeared at an upstairs window. 'Don't bother to come down,' said the bishop, 'as I am sure you must be busy', and when he found she was making a bed he insisted on helping her, commenting, 'I hate making beds. They always seem to come alive when I touch the sheets and blankets.' As he got to know the geography of the parsonages, it was his usual practice to make straight for the 'loo', sometimes without troubling to make his entry known to the incumbent.

When he came to the diocese practically no work was being done to the parsonages on account of the war. One vicar's wife took him upstairs and showed him water cascading through the ceiling of a bedroom. As she escorted the bishop to his car a few minutes later she saw that he was in

---

[1] A similar story is told of Russell when he was a much younger man. He was crossing a road in Manchester with his nose deep in a book and was nearly run down by a taxi. A torrent of abuse flowed from the driver's seat, to which Russell innocently replied, 'No thanks, old man, I don't want a taxi.'

tears. The next day he was on the phone to the archdeacon. 'Something must be done at once,' he shouted, 'I am not going to have my clergy living in pigsties.' He was told by the archdeacon that an aged rector and his wife had gone through the war with no interior lavatory. In all weathers they had to cross an outside yard when nature demanded. Although the war had been over several months, the authorities in Retford responsible for the issuing of licenses for repairs and improvements refused permission for an interior W.C. to be constructed. Russell pressed the patron, a noble Lord, to raise the matter in the House of Lords. The resistance of the local officials quickly melted away.

Although, on account of his increasing deafness, the bishop could hear very little that was said to him, he generally pretended that he had heard. His Malapropian replies were somewhat disconcerting until the clergy and their wives had grown accustomed to them. When the bishop was about to tour the United States in the early days of television, a vicar's wife asked him if he would be televised. The question had to be repeated several times. In the end the bishop answered rather wryly, 'Terrified, terrified, why should I be terrified?' Two teen-age girls were spending a night in Nottingham whilst their parents were moving house. They ran into the bishop who asked them where they lived. 'Please Sir,' answered one of the girls correctly, 'at the moment we don't live anywhere exactly.' 'Jolly nice place,' said the bishop, 'used to live there myself.' 'I was in the habit of storing up subjects of interest against his visits,' writes an incumbent who knew the bishop very well. 'Sometimes he took the bait at once and the float bobbed up and down once or twice and then suddenly he would withdraw, not into trivialities (of which he had no store), but behind *The Times* which I would put into his hands.'

Those who knew F. R. Barry and his contemporary B. K. Cunningham, the much-loved Principal of Westcott House, Cambridge, can hardly fail to compare the effect of almost complete deafness on their respective ministries. With Cunningham it was less of a handicap because he lived out his days in the confines of a compact theological college, meeting the same men day by day and mastering with them an intuitive technique of communication. Barry had to be much more out in the world, was confronted with new faces every day and forced into conversation with people who were not initially aware when they spoke to him that he could hear nothing they said. But the affliction Barry and Cunningham shared had this one effect on both of them. Their deafness became legendary, was the source of innumerable stories true and apocryphal, and aroused more affection than irritation, even though it could lead to embarrassing situations.

One thing the bishop never suggested to the clergy was that he knew how to do their job better than they did. 'The thing I admired about him most,' writes one of them, 'was that he let the clergy get on with their jobs.' He refrained from sitting in judgment on any of them, whatever he said about them in private. If he knew that a man had a tough job he might visit him three or four times a year but he never tried to prop up morale with pious platitudes. Rather the reverse. Standing in the middle of a noisy and rather out-of-hand youth club on a new housing estate, the bishop said to the vicar, 'You'll go mad if you stay here long, old boy. You must have a holiday.' The next day a cheque for £25 arrived from the bishop's discretionary fund, and when a few weeks later the bishop learnt that the young man had not yet taken advantage of the gift, he rang up to find out why he had not gone. With another incumbent in a similar situation, the bishop not only insisted on his going away, but went over to the parish to do duty during his absence. 'He was quite the nicest and most pastorally-minded bishop I ever knew,' wrote a parish priest of long experience.

III

At gatherings of the laity, who had not had the same opportunity as the clergy of getting the measure of the man, Russell was at first a complete mystery. At a civic ceremony in Nottingham he was told that a local worthy had died very suddenly that morning, 'Jolly good show,' said the bishop. At a party in his own house a vivacious lady who habitually gesticulated in conversation, thrust out her hand in the bishop's direction to illustrate a point in the middle of a long story. The bishop grasped it saying, 'So sorry you can't stop. Goodbye', and turned away. In summer he would often slip away and be found reading a paperback in the garden. At the reception after his archdeacon's wedding, he fell into a reverie during the speeches. Suddenly arousing himself and looking around he spotted quite a number of diocesan officials amongst the guests and, forgetting where he was, leant across to the bridegroom and boomed out, 'When is this ghastly affair going to end? If it doesn't finish soon, I'm off.' Lunching with a friend in a restaurant, he would cause some embarrassment by talking in a very loud voice. A dead silence would fall over all the other tables when the bishop's voice would be heard booming, 'Well, I hear the Archbishop has been making an ass of himself again.' At the end of his episcopate he and Lilian gave a series of farewell parties which tired the bishop almost to desperation. He slipped into a corner of the room, lay down on a sofa and went to sleep much to the consternation of the guests when they came to say goodbye. Yet in his dealings with people he was courteous and gentle and exercised over them a fascinating charm which they would be at pains to define. The half-smile which the girls at the Greycoat School had noticed a generation before, the flick of the tongue, the strange blend of pathos and impishness, melted the hearts of people who might have condemned his strange social behaviour in anyone else.

One characteristic of the bishop was that although he often emitted an inimitable guffaw, he was seldom heard to laugh. He had very little small talk. In the Nottingham County Club he was not at ease in a company which seemed to be chiefly interested in what was going on at Trent Bridge or at that week's point-to-point. He was not the sort of person whom his friends would have invited to come round to the local for 'a quick one'. 'Oh, isn't the bishop a dear,' said a very horsey young lady to the archdeacon. 'Of course he is completely out of touch with this world, isn't he?' To which the archdeacon replied, 'There is no one in the county more knowledgeable about what is going on in the world than the bishop.' He might have added, 'But perhaps he doesn't know as much as you would like him to do about your world of hunt balls and race meetings.'

Although he mystified the laity he often made a deep impression on them. At a solicitors' annual dinner he seemed to take little interest in the food that was put before him, nor in what was going on around him. During the speeches he seemed to be asleep. Then when it came to his turn to respond to the toast of the guests, according to one of the company present, he never missed a trick and fastened on to everything of interest that had been said previously. When, as was his custom, he left immediately after the speeches before the company had risen from the table, he was given a standing ovation. 'Your bishop—what a man!' commented a sidesman to his vicar the next morning.

With one organization in particular, Russell was at pains to cultivate the happiest relations. That was the Press. He himself was a born journalist. His younger brother, Sir Gerald Barry, the architect of the Festival of Britain, had been for a time the editor of the *News Chronicle.* 'Always be polite to the Press,' the bishop used to say when greatly irritated by it, 'they always have the last word.' With this sentiment in mind he bore patiently the importunities of press photographers who delayed him in the vestry before an institution and kept him waiting on cold nights outside the porch after the service. There were deep motives for the fostering of good relations. As his curates at St. John's had noticed, he often seemed to preach over the heads of the congregation to the world beyond. When preparing a sermon for a big occasion, he always had in mind the possibility of it being widely reported in the papers. His monthly letter in the *Southwell Diocesan News* appeared almost in full in the *Newark Advertiser.* When his particular brainchild, the *Southwell Review,* came to an end under financial pressure after six years life, the editor of *The Times* was one of those who wrote deploring its cessation.

After his brilliant academic career at Oxford and his successful pastorate at St. Mary's, Oxford, Russell naturally made a beeline for University College, Nottingham, which later achieved full university status. His first sermon after his enthronement was given at the College. He was a prime mover in establishing the divinity faculty there with its own professor and later a chaplaincy with pastoral responsibilities. He kept on very good terms with Bertrand Hallwood, the first Vice-Chancellor, and he was a constant visitor at all the social occasions, some of them of the kind he would have tried to avoid elsewhere.

Russell's interest in the schools in the diocese was general rather than particular. He liked young people, but until he had grandchildren of his own, he was not altogether at ease with them before they began to emerge from adolescence. He did not find talking to confirmation candidates easy, and he could never work up much enthusiasm over church schools, even though he encouraged parishes which possessed one to maintain its aided status. But it was felt with some justification that his concern for retaining a church school was largely strategic, prompted by the theory that the church could only retain a foothold in the state educational system if it still hung on to a number of its own schools. He was more interested in Christianizing state education generally than in providing 'sound Christian teaching' in a minority of protected schools.

Russell always said that he enjoyed visiting village churches for old time's sake. This may be true; but he did not really relish preaching in their pulpits to simple congregations. As the years rolled on and he became more tired, he took less and less trouble over his ordinary parochial sermons. He often started with a quip which set the congregation smiling, as when he instituted a new incumbent who had come from the diocese of Bath and Wells: 'Down in Somerset where Mr. Dunn comes from they don't mash tea, they drink cider.' Very often his sermon began with a reference to the weather, about which Russell had a strange obsession. In fact the weather in Nottinghamshire is rather more favourable than in many parts of the country, but Russell did not think so, perhaps because it was not till he became a bishop that he had to brave the elements day after day and night after night. Some of the curates used to keep a score of the number of references to the weather at the beginning of the bishop's sermons.

After the opening pleasantries the bishop tended to trail off into rather long and rambling discourses; a series of ideas as they came into his head. At an institution in a mining parish attended chiefly by the wives of tradesmen with hardly a miner's wife, let alone a coal-face worker, in the church, the bishop told his audience that it was not enough to make Christians out of miners—it was the Coal Board that they ought to make Christian. In his autobiography he admits quite candidly that confirmations wearied him and he was often thinking of something quite different during the actual service. The majority of the candidates in the Nottinghamshire parishes were of very different intellectual calibre from those he had prepared for confirmation at the Greycoat School, Westminster, and he could not bring himself to talk down to them. A parish priest writes, 'He dared to think widely, indeed was unable to do anything else. Hence instead of providing bible sermons which he could have done very well, he tried to push us out into wider fields where his thoughts ranged. It was one of his limitations that he did not realize that a lot of his hearers could not travel with him. He was careless of his preaching on ordinary occasions and did not prepare his sermons properly.' This was a pity because in the popular commentary on Ephesians, *A Philosophy from Prison,* he had shown how apt he could be in simple biblical exposition. Commenting on the words 'Let not the sun go down upon thy wrath' he had written, 'Real anger is a divine quality: bad temper and personal resentment are at best merely babyish . . . "be ye angry and sin not" means don't go to bed sulkily like silly children.' Congregations in the Southwell diocese could have done with more expositions of this sort from their bishop.

It would be an understatement to say that the bishop's demeanour in church tended to be unconventional. Once in the Minster when the canons were encircled around him and the choir were rendering a moving introit, the bishop, who was wearing cope and mitre, was seen to have one foot up on a sedilia as he did up a shoelace. On another occasion, the bishop arrived very late for a communion service, so late that the assistant bishop was asked to begin without him. When finally he arrived, unaware how late he was, he found the congregation standing for the Gospel and thinking it was as a mark of respect to himself, he shouted from the door, 'Oh, do sit down, do sit down.'

IV

Russell was at his best at gatherings of the clergy, especially at their annual conference at Swanwick and also when giving the presidential address at diocesan conferences when the laity were given the opportunity of discovering for themselves, what their bishop was capable of delivering. From a rich treasury of things old and new he gave them prophecy of the first order, spiced and made all the more palatable with typical Barryian quips. He never went to retreats himself. 'I get bored stiff with a voice going on and on like a dripping tap' he once confessed, and he would resist all efforts to get him to give a purely devotional address. His arch-deacons once succeeded in persuading him much against his will to give one at Swanwick. The bishop began as if he really was going to do what he had been asked to do but soon reverted to his usual prophetic style. His replies to questions could be brutally down to earth on occasions. An elderly clergyman who had a bee in his bonnet about birth control asked the bishop at a conference, 'My Lord, what would you say to a girl in your church if you found she was employed in a factory making contraceptives?' Realizing that he was faced with a very mixed audience, the bishop's reply was unexpectedly evasive, but afterwards he said to a friend privately, 'What I wanted to say to ————— was, "Tell her that she should make the things as carefully as possible. Many a marriage has foundered as a result of a faulty one".' It should be added that the bishop was never heard to tell a risqué story for the sake of it, and no-one ever dared to tell him one.

Partly on account of his deafness and also because of his disinclination to be drawn into administration, the bishop was at his weakest when chairing meetings. The diocesan conference sometimes became pantomimic, with the archdeacons sitting each side of him roaring out the questions which had come up from the floor. Someone had moved a motion. There was a prolonged silence. An archdeacon tip-toed up to the bishop and shouted into his ear, 'My Lord, will you put the motion?' 'What is the motion?' replied the bishop wearily, as one waking from sleep. On the other hand his deafness could sometimes be employed to his own advantage. He could switch off his hearing aid in the middle of a dull speech, apparently unaware that the screeching sounds which were emitted from it gave away to everyone, including the speaker, what the bishop was up to. A rural dean, who ought to have known better, spun out a very long question of the sort that bored the unfortunate bishop stiff. It was something to do with a vicar who consistently absented himself from chapter meetings. 'What would you do with such a man?' implored the rural dean with deep emotion. The bishop who had pretended to be listening and on whose face patience and agony were written in equal proportions, briefly cut in with, 'I couldn't agree with you more, George, old boy. Back the Mothers' Union up to the hilt every time. Now let's get on with the next business.'

The bishop's deafness induced in him a timidity which was really foreign to his nature. He was embarrassed by verbal confrontations which he could tell from the expression on the face of the speaker were intended unpleasantly. He was vulnerable at diocesan conferences to members who were critical of diocesan policy. Yet in spite of this vulnerability only two or three clerics and hardly any laymen ever took advantage of their bishop's weaknesses during the length of his episcopate. This in itself speaks volumes for the affection and respect in which he was held. 'Do I look like a sergeant-major?' he retorted amidst roars of laughter to a member of the diocesan conference who accused the diocese, and by implication the bishop, of some high-handed action.

For some reason Russell was allergic to staff meetings which in most dioceses take place monthly and are fixed in advance at the beginning of the year. In Southwell they occurred very infrequently and then only after the archdeacons had made it clear to the bishop that diocesan administration would come to a standstill if one was not held. Towards the end of his episcopate when the bishop had become old, tired, and sad, his policy of delegation, which originally had been a healthy feature of his episcopate, amounted almost to abdication. For a long time he had left the filling of livings of what he regarded as of minor importance to the archdeacons who would be amused when, at the institution, the bishop would announce to the congregation what a great deal of trouble he had taken over the appointment. 'Would you like me to get on with finding a man, Bishop?' an archdeacon would say. 'I wish you would, old boy,' the bishop would reply, turning back again to his desk. There was, of course, some grumbling amongst the clergy in the diocese at what they aptly described as 'this presbyterian form of government', and eyebrows were raised when in order to set the archdeacons free from parochial responsibilities quite a large sum of money had to be allocated to augmenting their stipends to replace their benefice incomes and to accommodate them in private houses. In those days archdeacons were expected to hold benefices, and Southwell was one of the first dioceses to set its archdeacons free exclusively for diocesan duties.

Very little of the bishop's correspondence now survives. Perhaps this is an advantage to his biographer because his handwriting was so nearly illegible that his correspondents were often unable to decipher it. Professor Trevelyan admitted that he had been so busy writing books that he had never tried to develop an attractive epistolary style. The same may be true of Russell. However, a letter survives from this period which shows his sympathy for parents bereaved by the loss of a son in battle. The boy had fallen at Alamein:

> 'It will help I think to feel that his life has been given as part of the cost of a victory which may be the beginning of liberation for the world, not in an abortive or disastrous "defensive". But that will not heal broken hearts. He did not "lose" his life. He gave it and so finds it in life eternal. Don't you feel that all the experience of this time thrusts the eternal hope of Christianity into the very centre of our faith as the one thing that makes sense of life and reveals victory and fulfilment in the heart of pain? May it be so with you and may you hear the trumpets on the other side.'

His letters to the clergy in answer to requests for advice were brief, to the point, friendly, and completely devoid of the pomposities and pieties which some dignitaries have inflicted on correspondents. 'I don't suppose God minds,' he replied to a P.C.C. member who complained that the vicar was in the habit of bringing his dog into church.

V

With his staff Russell maintained happy, in some cases deeply affectionate, relationships. At St. Mary's, Nottingham, he found Bishop Neville Talbot who had been a very successful high-ranking chaplain in the first world war and had gone on to be a bishop in Africa. Neville was a scion of the historic family of Talbot which in the Middle Ages had a reputation for being a law unto itself. He himself was the product of an age which encouraged distinctive characters. In every respect he was a giant of a man. When he returned to England from Africa, the authorities were never able to find him a place suitable for his powerful personality and great abilities, and he had to be content with St. Mary's, Nottingham, which he combined with the assistant bishopric. Perhaps his unpredictable behaviour and what in other people would have been regarded as outrageous utterances account for his never being offered further preferment. Russell himself used to tell how in the officers' mess at G.H.Q. in France, 'Brasshats' after a somewhat alcoholic evening, were greeted over their breakfasts next morning by Neville with a clap on the back and 'Your wouldn't be looking like that this morning if you had said your prayers before going to bed last night.'

Neville and Russell could not have been more different in physique and character. The bishop must have been aware that his assistant was at heart a disappointed man and that it would not be altogether easy for him to accept as his diocesan one who had been so much his junior in France. But Neville was too much of a gentleman and a Christian ever to reveal any resentments. Both men had a mutual respect and affection for one another, and their partnership which ended with Neville's sudden death three years later, just before he was due to leave the diocese to be episcopal chaplain to the R.A.F., was a very happy one.

In W. J. Conybeare and J. P. Hales, Russell inherited a provost and an archdeacon of charm, grace, and dignity. At the turn of the century Conybeare had been chaplain to Archbishop Frederick Temple and in that capacity had attended the coronation of King Edward VII when Russell was twelve years of age. Hales had been ordained by Bishop Ridding, the first bishop of Southwell, who had been his headmaster at Winchester. For Ridding, Hales had a respect which amounted almost to worship. A keen cricketer and sportsman, he claimed, surely with some exaggeration, that he had shot a partridge in every field in Nottinghamshire. He too had been a high-ranking army chaplain, senior to his new bishop, and like Russell, had been awarded the D.S.O. These two patricians found their new bishop very different from Dr. Mosley, who was a dignitary out of the same mould as themselves. But from the beginning they recognized Russell's great qualities and were appreciative of his tactful understanding of their long established status in the diocese. In spite of the fact that Russell was essentially an intellectual, he always had a warm place in his heart for the gentlemen in holy orders, the grown-up edition of the 'good chap about the quad' of his own college days.

When Conybeare retired, the bishop appointed Hugh Heywood, Dean of Caius College, Cambridge, to be Provost of Southwell. Heywood was an ex-regular army officer, a few years younger than Russell, and had gone up to Cambridge rather late. Nevertheless he carried off two Firsts and some University prizes. Like his bishop, he was an excellent classics and New Testament scholar. He had a clear quick brain; in fact many people found it alarmingly quick. He never suffered fools gladly and was unaware of his tremendous intellectual strength when in verbal combat with contestants less agile than himself. At heart he was a kind man and a good pastor when his sympathies were aroused, which they often were. Of all the diocesan staff, he was least tolerant of his bishop's weaknesses. He was still Provost of Southwell when Russell retired.

It was the bishop's habit to bring to key positions in the diocese men who were not in the prime of life. They had not reached it. He was naturally drawn to younger men and was happy to work with them. What the archdeacons of his appointment may have lacked in experience they made up for in energy. It was, perhaps, too clear that Russell had a preference for graduates from Oxford and Cambridge. As was to be expected, his appointment of young men from outside the diocese did not go without criticism from some senior men who had served in it for years. In defence of his policy it can be said that he always kept his best goods in the front of the shop window where they attracted the attention of passers-by. If he had a good man worthy of promotion, he did not hide the fact from other bishops, even at the risk of losing him. As a result of this generosity, not shared by all other contemporary bishops, more clergy from the diocese of Southwell were promoted to bishoprics, deaneries and archdeaconries than from any other diocese at that time.

Russell was very fortunate in his part-time chaplains, all of whom were country parsons in the neighbourhood of Southwell. Nicholas Allenby, a Kelham father, who had been nursemaid to his literary baby, the *Southwell Review,* became his spiritual director and the closest to him of all his staff. Nicholas stood by the bishop in his moments of depression and ministered to him during his last illness. Russell also leant heavily for spiritual support on Morris Gelsthorpe, Gwynne's successor as Bishop of the Sudan, whom he brought to the diocese as assistant bishop and rector of Bingham.

VI

Composing his monthly letter for the diocesan leaflet gave the bishop more satisfaction than most other duties that fell to him. Episcopal letters in diocesan journals too often give the impression that they are composed in great haste after an urgent telephone message from the editor that he will be calling round for the material in twenty minutes. Over twenty-two years Russell maintained a standard of writing which compares favourably with leading articles in *The Times.* The *Southwell Review* was the best diocesan quarterly of its time and in the same literary class as Henson's *Bishopric* in the diocese of Durham. In it he reviewed books which had interested him and commented on contemporary events which were hitting the headlines in the press. 'God rest you, merry gentlemen' was the title of his first Christmas letter in 1941 when the news from the war front was consistently bad. When petrol rationing became tight the bishop warned that many committees would have to be curtailed. 'It is up to us to prove that the Church can exist without so many committees. Will that be altogether a bad thing?' he asked. After thirty years of increasing bureaucracy in Church and State, we can today appreciate the pertinence of the bishop's question. When the Beveridge Report, the blueprint of the Welfare State, about which Russell was to have so much to say after the war, was published in 1943, he pointed out, 'This was not a revolution but the application and systematizing of legislation that has been going on ever since the beginning of the century.' Then followed words of warning which the general public would have done well to heed in the years of affluence after the war: 'The Welfare State will not be paid for out of some magical goldmine. Government money is our money raised by taxes. The Welfare State needs sacrifice and dedication on the part of the whole nation if it is to work.' Like most of his contemporaries, he was wrong in his prophecy that the twenty-five years after the war would be years of austerity. They were in fact affluent years beyond his wildest dreams.

At the beginning of 1945 when it was becoming clear that victory in the West was just around the corner, Russell warned his readers of the sacrifices that would have to be made if the country was to be as successful in establishing peace as it had been in winning the war. He linked these thoughts with the report *Towards the Conversion of England* which was being commended to parochial study groups throughout the country and had attracted a great deal of attention. Never since his days at St. Mary's a great money-raiser, he backed the diocesan appeal which set as its target the sum of £150,000 to augment the stipends of the clergy, which at that time averaged about £500 and were recognized as being quite unrealistic in view of inflation.

In June 1945 a month after the end of the war, he quoted Churchill, 'The price of victory is a share in shaping the pattern of the future.' It had probably not dawned on the Prime Minister, certainly not on the Bishop of Southwell, how greatly British power in the world was to be reduced and how small a part, compared with the past, it was to play in the shaping of a new world in the years that lay ahead. Meanwhile the General Election began to absorb the attention of the population. The bishop warned his clergy not to sit on political platforms although they must exercise their right to vote. 'The parson is the parson of the whole parish and must not take sides in matters of public controversy.'

Compared with his mood in 1919 Russell struck a more sober note. In 1945 he visited the Army of Occupation on the Rhine and saw for himself the dreadful devastation of the German cities by allied bombing. He also detected signs of demoralization in the population, perhaps not realizing fully how great are the Teutonic powers of recuperation. 'Every report that comes into us from Europe shows how mortal the danger is still that civilization may break down altogether. England alone has preserved the continuity of her own life and institutions.' It was at this time, a month after V.E.

Day, that Russell was preaching in Westminster Abbey. With justifiable pride, considering the part he had played in its rescue five years before, he opened his sermon with a toss of his head and a typical gesture of his arms: 'Well, the Abbey stands!' A month later he wrote in his letter, 'The country has now the opportunity to be the rallying-point for the revival of those permanent and essential values for which Western civilization has always stood.'

At the end of the year Russell was clearly wondering if the country was in a fit state to respond to the challenge. Quoting from the Advent Collect, he wrote, 'It is high time to awake out of sleep.' The war with the Japanese had come to an end four months before. On the atom bomb he wrote, 'It calls for a re-interpretation of the meaning of human life. Power has broken loose from moral control. Human life has become the slave of power. If we cannot bring it back under moral control and make it again the servant of human purpose, we shall be annihilated by it. That is our mission to the world.' There is no mention here of Russia and the imminence of the Cold War.

Russell's method of presenting his message was existential. He began by describing some contemporary trend or event of which his readers would all be aware and then would show how it revealed the underlying human tragedy. He would point out the inadequacy of purely secularist and humanistic interpretations of the human situation and man's inability to solve his own problems. Then according to the season of the year he would suddenly drive home the Christian message. At the beginning of Lent: 'Against that background [the affluent society] will you reflect on the story of the Temptation in the Wilderness?' One December he wrote, 'Advent is not about a remote and receding future. It is about what God is doing now.'

Many people within the diocese and even more outside it in many parts of the world avidly read everything Russell wrote in his diocesan publication. It is understandable that many of the readers of the diocesan leaflet which was enclosed each month in parish magazines, who normally looked for pious tit-bits, did not find their bishop's letter altogether congenial. There seemed to be a certain monotony in the constant repetition of such expressions as 'the inadequacy of the purely humanistic interpretation of life'; 'the bankruptcy of secularism' and even the often-repeated three words, 'the living God' of whom they were told by the bishop they were in such need. People who did not read *The Times* leading articles— and they were the majority of the clientele of parish magazines—found the bishop's writings too strong meat for them. Clergy complained that demand for the diocesan leaflet dropped. When one lady told her vicar that it wasn't worth 3d. the vicar tartly replied, 'The bishop's letter to you each month is worth considerably more than that. I would point out that there are people throughout the world who buy anything and everything he writes, for he is in the true line of prophecy (which means forth-telling). Keep those letters for twelve months and fasten them together and you will have a brochure which, if published as such, would earn praises and commendations from the reviewer. We are privileged people.' This indeed was true, but unfortunately the majority of church-goers do not rate prophecy and scholarship high amongst a bishop's qualifications and are not in the habit of reading reviews.

'Conversation,' wrote Gibbon, 'enriches the understanding. Isolation is the school of genius.' One of Russell's clergy wrote of him, 'He lived in his mind and he lived alone there. What went on was recorded in his books and articles.' As everyone who has tried to write a book knows only too well, an author becomes very jealous of his privacy and is resentful of interruptions. 'Merciless, merciless,' Russell would mutter as he dragged himself from his desk and groped his way to the garage in order to do a confirmation or institution. It was a pity he grumbled so much about the miseries of episcopacy when he was out of the diocese because it gave the impression to those who did not know him well that he must be an ineffective bishop. Probably he never fully realized what a lot of time he allowed for writing. When a vicar went to see him one day in his study, he asked the bishop if he had seen a new book by a brother bishop. 'I can't think how these bishops ever find time to write books,' replied Russell, apparently unaware that at that very moment he was correcting the proofs of one of his own.

VII

There was one activity of its bishop, an important one, which largely escaped the notice of the diocese because generally it was only briefly reported in the local press. This was his participation in the debates in the House of Lords. The Lords symbolized for Russell that close relationship between Church and State which was so dear to him. He had, however, to wait seven years after his consecration before he took his seat[1] and then only made his maiden speech on 17 May 1950. Some bishops experience difficulty in acclimatizing themselves to the atmosphere of the Upper House. Long before they get there they are well initiated into the art of speaking on platforms and in the pulpit to captive audiences, and those who were academics are conditioned to the lecture room. But the Lords Spiritual must at all costs resist the temptation to lecture or to preach at their fellow peers. Even though their speeches may be prepared with great care and the subject that they are dealing with is a weighty one, it is well for them to adopt a rather casual and confidential manner which some bishops have seemed incapable of acquiring. In this respect Russell was eminently successful. His speeches were prepared with the greatest care and there is little doubt that he spent the evening before their delivery rehearsing them in his bedroom at the Royal Commonwealth Society. His manner was such as to commend him to his fellow peers.

Unlike some of his brother bishops, Russell was not disposed to leap to his feet either in Convocation or the Church Assembly on every occasion, whatever the subject under debate happened to be. In the Lords he bided his time and waited until inspiration came to him, then carefully mastered his subject and delivered his speech without a trace of nervousness, but throughout with becoming modesty. After his maiden speech he was warmly congratulated by the Duke of Montrose who expressed the hope that the Right Reverend Prelate would often be heard on future occasions. In fact it was nearly four years before he rose to speak again and in the

[1] Since the 1830s the number of bishoprics has been increased but the number of seats allocated to the bishops has remained the same as it was before the creation of the new sees. Bishops other than the two Archbishops and the bishops of London, Winchester and Durham have to wait their turn to take their seats.

fourteen years he was in the Lord's he only spoke ten times. His increasing deafness prevented him from making many new friends there.

Russell's rare speeches were a model of what an episcopal contribution to the debates should be. They rank amongst some of his best literary efforts. The subjects on which he chose to speak reveal the catholicity of his interests. He addressed the House when some great moral issue was involved, as in the debate on 19 May 1954 when the laws relating to homosexuality were under consideration. His interest in young people came out on several occasions, as when there was a motion moved by Lord Stansgate[1] that the Boy Scout movement, with its promise of loyalty to God and the King, should open its doors to professed atheists and communists. He took part in the debates on the Albemarle Report and, on 18 May 1960, on the Children and Young Person's Bill. He spoke twice on matters which particularly concerned his own diocese: subsidence by coal mining, when he began by reminding the House, 'We know a lot about coal in Nottinghamshire' and then when referring to the roadsign 'DANGER—BEWARE OF ROAD SUBSIDENCE' he compared the fate awaiting motorists with that of Dathan and Abiram.[2] On 19 February 1958 he played a prominent part in the debate on the reform of the laws relating to mental illness, championing the staff of Rampton Hospital in his diocese which had come under some heavy criticism in the last few months. He spoke of the isolation from the rest of the community, referring to the hospital as more of a map reference than a place. He had done his homework and had thoroughly mastered the subject. He reminded the Lords that it was the system under which the staff worked, not any shortcomings of their own, which ought to be blamed for defects in the hospital.

Russell's political philosophy comes out very clearly in many of his speeches, particularly in one in a debate on the powers of the Cabinet. He had voted Tory since the 1920s but by temperament was a Liberal. He was always on the watch for infringement of civil liberties. 'How can a strong government avoid overwhelming the liberties which it is trying to defend without demoralizing the country it is trying to serve?' he asked. He went on to deplore the modern tendency, particularly in local government, 'to turn everything into politics always by feeding the insatiable appetite of the State at the expense of the community on which it rests.' 'The really effective bulwark against central power is the vigour and the jealous independence of all those subordinate societies, local government, clubs, associations of all kinds, professional guilds, trade organizations, cultural foundations and, above all, the primary group, the family, which make the total community on which the State depends.' To this list he might have added the House of Lords itself which even then was regarded by some political radicals as an impediment to democracy but which, as many of the debates in which Russell took part demonstrate clearly, is one of the guarantors of it. When Russell spoke on centralized power in 1950 the threat of the 'closed shop' and of other aspects of organized labour to the constitution was not as apparent as it is today. Russell ended his speech with the words, 'The whole Christian philosophy of politics on which

1 Father of Mr. Anthony Wedgwood Benn.
2 In Numbers 16 the earth opened up to swallow Abiram and Dathan as a punishment for offending Moses.

Western Europe has been founded has always taken for granted that the State itself is under the law answerable to a higher law which no state makes and no state can presume to alter. The modern state tends more and more to claim to be the source and creator of law rather than its guardian and interpreter.' And then in words which exactly sum up his attitude towards the place of religion in the community, 'Freedom in our tradition and our inheritance has always been bound up with and dependent upon what I call a religious valuation of men and women.'

In the debate on the Children and Young Person's Bill in November 1962, Russell took the opportunity of making it clear what he thought should be the attitude of the Church to the Welfare State. 'The Church can never again have a monopoly in the social services. It ought never to wish to have it. There is something wrong with the Church which wishes to dominate. The Church, like Christianity itself, ought to go into every situation not to be ministered unto but to minister.' But he then added, 'You can't measure the influence of the Church simply by counting heads on Sundays. What is called diffused Christianity is a very real force.' He believed that a partnership between the Welfare State, the Church, and the voluntary bodies, was essential. On 12 March 1963, in a debate on racial problems and education, Russell made a plea for this country to accept the challenge of the presence of coloured people in its midst, 'by making itself a model of trans-racial relationships. Multi-racialism is going to be the norm everywhere. The Empire,' he added pithily, 'is coming home'. He then turned to the part that schools should play in this matter. 'Children', he argued, 'have no anti-racialism till adults put it into their heads. The schools should provide by their general character as well as by specific teaching the climate for true liberality.' He admitted that it is the 'mixed-up kid' that gets involved in race riots and that there is a psychosis which cannot be banished by one R.E. lesson a week and by a few words at morning assembly. 'It can be discouraged,' he concluded, 'by the whole tone of the school.'

In a debate on 18 May 1960 on the Albemarle Report, Russell revealed his special concern and interest in young people and the amount of time that he had given to reports from the clergy on the new housing estates in his diocese and from his youth chaplains. He had then turned seventy. Young people, he told his fellow peers, get into trouble in the urban areas because they have nothing to do. He was making a plea for some financial aid for clubs. He cited the failure complex which afflicted many children when they failed the eleven plus: 'Debilitated by a sense of guilt, embittered by a feeling of resentment, they are trying to find some significance in life in their tribal cults and aggressive behaviour, or to get their own back and take revenge in violent crime. The so-called Teddy Boys are the status-seekers in our mainly quantitative society which hardly has any room or status for persons as persons.'

Russell's contribution to the debate on the proposed revision of the laws on homosexuality reveals a curious ambivalence in his attitude to the subject which in some respects put him ahead of many of his contemporaries and in other respects behind his juniors. Russell was a product of the Victorian Public School in which homosexual practices were regarded as a grievous and detestable offence, to be suppressed with force or expulsion

'FRB', Bishop of Southwell, 1951

'FRB' with the, Archbishop of Grodno, 1947

'FRB', saying his office a month before his death, 1976

and, in the case of adults, by terms of imprisonment. For people of Russell's generation, homosexuality was the unmentionable vice. So when he addressed the Lords with 'reluctance' and 'repugnance' on a subject which was very distasteful to many of his audience, he maintained that homosexual relationships were a moral evil and sinful to the highest degree. Admittedly, he was speaking with the voice of the past. But he continued with a voice which belonged more to the future and which many of his hearers in 1954 must have regarded as highly permissive, when he advocated an objective enquiry into whether or not the law should be amended to free consenting adults from prosecution. 'There is little to suggest that a prison sentence succeeds in reforming an offender who,' Russell added, 'was to be pitied rather than punished.' Finally he protected himself against any suggestion of behaviourism by strongly deploring the attitude of mind betrayed in the plea, 'I am not a free and responsible moral agent. I am made that way. It is not my fault. I cannot help it.' By the grace of God, Russell asserted, a homosexual can triumph over his disabilities.

Russell spoke on two other occasions, once in a debate on road accidents when he advocated an absolute speed limit of 60 m.p.h. for all vehicles at all times, and again on a motion moved by Lord Arran that this chamber welcomes attempts which are being made in the direction of Christian unity; a strange debate for the House of Lords, the propriety of which some members questioned and Archbishop Fisher tried unsuccessfully to quash. Russell spoke in support of the motion with hesitation, for he feared that the subject was one which might encourage the bishops 'to hog the microphone'. One of the things he valued in the House of Lords was its secularity, always making his Christianity stand out more by implication than by overt assertion. In this debate his latent anti-clericalism came through, as it had done in his articles from the trenches in 1917. He had always been critical of assemblies in which clergy predominated. He was aware that in the end clerics can only get away with what the laity allow them. On this occasion he told their Lordships that it was up to the laity to storm the barriers between the different denominations which in the past they had allowed the cleric to raise and to maintain.

VIII

Russell was subject to periods of depression amounting sometimes almost to despair. He therefore needed, over and above his normal devotional exercises, something to take him out of himself and he found it in his chalet, 'The Coppice', at Manesty in Borrowdale which he shared with Harry Baines, his former curate at St. Mary's, Oxford. He was ravished by the wide open spaces of the lakeland, the scent of the heather and the fragrance of the flowers in spring. All this provided him with the refreshment he needed and also charged his batteries for further literary effort. A friend who climbed with him to the summit of Great Gable described the experience as being like accompanying Moses to the top of Mount Pisgah. He took advantage of the company of friends to speak as if to them, but as he was carried away, he became almost oblivious of them.

Russell was a compulsive traveller. In his early days he had entertained a vocation to serve the Church overseas, and it was this that had prompted him to accept Bishop Gwynne's invitation to go to Egypt in 1924. The war put an end to overseas travel until 1945 when he toured the British Army on the Rhine. Between 1950 and 1963 he went overseas on an average once every two years, always in the company of his wife, and latterly under her auspices after she became President of the Girls' Friendly Society. They returned to Australia and New Zealand which they had visited last in 1934. In 1952 he visited the States for the first time. His reputation had gone ahead of him and he found synods, colleges, and clergy-schools, agog to hear what he had got to say. When he first appeared on the platform his slight and, at a distance, not very impressive appearance came as a surprise, but he only had to speak a few words before he had rivetted attention upon himself. In 1961 he made an extensive tour of Africa. Russell described these tours modestly in the *Diocesan News* on his return, but they made a deep impression on the younger churches overseas. Perhaps it is not surprising that the diocese which he left in the hands of elderly assistant bishops and youthful archdeacons became somewhat critical of his frequent absences.

In the central councils of the Church, Russell's voice was heard less frequently than might have been expected. The disadvantage of establishing a great name in one generation is that one may be regarded as something of an anticlimax in the next. This was true of some of the priests who came to the forefront of the Church under war conditions. It was not true of Russell. His mind remained amazingly fertile. He continued to read and to write and it was largely through his books that his name was kept before the public. He played an important part in the 1948 Lambeth Conference when there was still a number of bishops of the same vintage as himself in the company. Ten years later he played a lesser part but when he did speak it was on vocation and the provision of fit persons for the ministry.

In Convocation and Church Assembly he spoke all too infrequently in the opinion of the proctors from his own diocese, who knew very well what he was capable of delivering. They were disconcerted by the pathetic appearance that he seemed deliberately to affect in the corridors which they suspected would be misunderstood by a generation that had not known him in his prime. When he did speak he could count on immediate attention.

Like many elderly men, Russell harboured the illusion that the rising generation was inferior to its predecessors. It may be true that there were few men of the calibre of his friends and contemporaries, like Leslie Hunter, Mervyn Haigh and John Rawlinson on the bench, but it really was not quite fair or accurate to describe the new generation of bishops as 'pygmies'. He had been Randall Davidson's bright-eyed boy. He had worked alongside William Temple and had been a close friend of Garbett. With Geoffrey Fisher he had less sympathy. Fisher was greatly taken up with the revision of the canons and Russell did not conceal his boredom with the whole project. Fisher was a brilliant administrator but no prophet, and always gave the impression that a doubt had never so much as crossed his mind. In the course of his life Russell had flirted with doubt. So much for Lambeth. At York Garbett had invited the diocesan bishops to Bishopthorpe in turn during the sessions of Convocation, but Russell was privileged with a standing invitation all of his own. Garbett's successor was a generation younger and had not known him in his prime. The privilege was no longer extended to Russell and he had to take his turn with the others. He cut rather a pathetic figure when he began to appear once more after nearly ten years in the halls and on the staircases of the Station Hotel.

In the diocese he was chiefly stirred by projects which had in them the semblance of novelty and adventure. A few months after V.E. Day he was delighted to address a number of German prisoners-of-war in a camp near Mansfield, some of whom intended to take up theological training on their return to the Fatherland. He felt he was doing something to help restore Germany as a Christian democracy. The new housing estates which sprang up like mushrooms around Nottingham, Mansfield and Worksop, captured his imagination, in particular Clifton to which he appointed Stephen Verney[1] who had been a 'cloak and dagger' agent behind the German lines in Greece during the war, and seemed to have all the qualifications for what Russell regarded as a pioneering adventure in evangelism. Princess Margaret, then President of the Church of England Youth Council, came to visit the estate and had lunch in a council house before going on to Southwell to take part in the Millenary celebrations of the Minister. The Church on these new housing estates seemed to be getting off to a flying start. At Clifton members of the congregation helped to put up the building and hardly a week went by without some reference to it in the Nottingham press. Russell prophesied that here was to be found a return to first century Christianity. But he was to be disappointed. The majority of the church people on the estates had grown up in traditional urban parishes in the heart of the city, and did not see themselves in the role suggested for them by their bishop. They wanted to reproduce the kind of church in their new surroundings such as they were accustomed to before the war. Some local residents obstinately refused to attend the new building because 'it did not look like a church', and chose to return to the city centre by bus to worship.

When Russell came to the diocese, party suspicion was rife amongst the clergy in Nottingham. The cause of this unfortunate state of affairs was largely historical. When, as a consequence of the Industrial Revolution, the population of the city rapidly expanded and poured over the medieval boundaries into the neighbouring fields, new churches had to be built and new parishes created. Unfortunately the patronage of many of these new benefices fell almost immediately into the hands of party trusts, most of them evangelical, whose main purpose was to provide a pastorate which could be trusted to keep the party flag flying. To the detriment of church life in Nottingham this they were very successful in doing, with the result that many of the clergy were hardly on speaking terms. When the announcement of Russell's appointment to the See of Southwell was made, a message went out to the evangelicals that their new bishop should be regarded with suspicion.

In the rural areas, partisan suspicion amongst the clergy existed, but was not nearly so widespread as in Nottingham. Country people do not take kindly to extremes in churchmanship. It is the eclectic congregation in the urban areas which can afford the luxury of particularity. But in north Nottinghamshire the seventh Duke of Newcastle who died in 1928 and was one of the three great ducal landowners in the north of the county had,

[1] Now Bishop of Repton.

71

for nearly half a century, exercised considerable influence in Church affairs through his extensive ecclesiastical patronage. An extreme high churchman, he built on his Clumber estate a magnificent church in the neo-gothic style, complete with aumbries, pyxes, and confessional boxes. When one of the benefices in his gift fell vacant, he habitually filled it with a priest of his own persuasion as likely as not with no previous experience of the rural ministry. Most of his clerical clients he discovered in the East end of London. So it was that in the place of the traditional homespun English parson with whom the villagers of Nottinghamshire were familiar, there emerged from the vicarages in the Duke's gift clergy arrayed in birettas and soutanes, such as were to be seen on the Continent, who, without consultation with their parishioners, introduced into the church all the ecclesiastical paraphernalia which the complacent Winnington-Ingram had allowed to run riot in his chaotic diocese. The Duke ensured that his patronage policy would continue after his death by handing over the advowsons to an anglo-catholic trust called 'The Society for the Maintenance of the Faith'. The clergy of the Duke's appointment came to be known as 'the North Road Rebels'. They too were warned to keep their distance from their new father-in-God, advice which it was not difficult for them to follow because it had long been their habit to refer to the Roman Catholic Bishop of Nottingham as 'our Bishop'.

Before long the extremists on both wings of the Church began to discover with surprise, perhaps in some cases not unmixed with disappointment, that their bishop had no intention of persecuting them. It was perhaps as well that they did not overhear his sly comments on their extravagances which he made in the privacy of his study. But when he called on them he invariably treated them with courtesy and consideration. As in so many other matters Russell had long accepted the fact that part of the peculiar charm of the Church of England was its likeness to a greenhouse in which exotic plants flourish alongside vegetation more robust and fruitful. He was to say in his farewell address that a bishop must be the 'appreciative and understanding Father in God to all. They are all his flock and they all belong to the Church and, what is more, the Church of England needs all of them to retain its character.' By the time he left the diocese he had not only allayed the suspicions of all but the most fanatical amongst his clergy but had also drawn the sting from the animosities which had divided them on his arrival 23 years before.

The fruit of Russell's gentle, wise and conciliatory handling of his clergy was best exemplified in the house parties held in three successive years over which he and Lilian presided at the Butlin's Camp in Skegness. Initially Russell intended to run them as conventional clerical conferences complete with services, lectures, and seminars, but after the first he decided to abandon these attempts to improve the shining hour, encouraging the clergy to bring their wives and families with them and to make the lectures voluntary. He told them that he just wanted them to enjoy themselves and get to know one another. This policy paid rich dividends. It drew the diocese together as a family and Russell, who had always preferred to play the part of Big Brother to the clergy, suddenly realized rather late in his episcopate that they had taken him to their hearts as Father-in-God. Some of the clergy had disapproved of Butlin's as a venue for a clerical houseparty but Russell persuaded them that it was very good for them to meet in such secular surroundings where many of their parishioners came for their annual holiday. Of course, a Butlin's holiday camp was the last place he himself would have chosen for a private holiday. On arrival he took one look at it, turned to the shore from which the tide had receded, and murmured 'the sea saw that and fled.' (Ps. 114.3). But for the rest of the week he seemed to be enjoying himself in the company of the clergy more than at any time in his episcopate.

On 22 June 1963, Russell gave his last presidential address to the diocesan conference. If the diocese had become a little restive about his deferred retirement many of those who heard him on this occasion must have felt that it was worth waiting for and fully compensated for their impatience. As an episcopal swansong it was a masterpiece. He kept the emotional temperature low, but throughout he spoke with affection and an obvious appreciation of the confidence which had been established between him and his flock. He spoke hopefully of the growing together of the various parties in the Church of England and added, 'Don't forget that there are three not two, the Catholic, the Reformed and the Liberal. Freedom of thought is the life-blood of our Church and we shall not remain what we are without it, and it may be said to be our most valuable and characteristic contribution to Christendom.' He could not resist a last tilt at the revision of the canons which had bored him so in Convocation. 'Some of them are just too silly to be printed,' he said, and then singled out one for particular castigation. This was the canon dealing with the vesture of the celebrant at Holy Communion. 'I find it difficult to believe that the Almighty minds much what we wear in church or out of it . . . all this fuss about clothes.'

This was the year of *Honest to God* which was to cause such a furore in the Church but which Russell took in his stride. He was in a strong position to speak a steadying word to the diocese at this moment of theological explosion. His own faith was grounded in traditional orthodoxy, but he had always championed those who were prepared to experiment with their theology. His last words urged the diocese not to keep the faith 'wrapped up in mothballs of unthinking and uncritical traditionalism'—vintage F.R.B.

During the last year in the diocese, Russell and Lilian and Rosemary suffered a grievous blow. Rosemary's husband died in an accident near the family home in the Lake District. The F. R. Barry of the Somme rose to the occasion. He cared for his stricken family with great tenderness and in what he wrote and spoke during this period he made a greater impression on the diocese than ever before. If sometimes his faith had appeared to be somewhat cerebral, people now saw it as the staff and support of his life. Once again it was proved in action.

It was now clear that his retirement would not be long delayed. During the summer he damaged his back in a fall whilst on holiday in Borrowdale and was therefore not able to take as full a part in the farewell gatherings that were arranged in his and Lilian's honour. Perhaps he was inwardly relieved because he was spared the strain that they would have imposed on his emotions. He ceased to be Bishop of Southwell on St. Luke's Day, 1963.

8. RETIREMENT

I

Russell dreaded retirement from the moment that the prospect of it loomed on the horizon. In his biography of Mervyn Haigh, he wrote:

'I have known a number of retired bishops and nearly all of them have been unhappy. The break with their past is so shatteringly complete. A retired bishop must leave his diocese (as every parson must leave his parish) and cut himself off from all the friendships formed in it and few men have so many as a bishop has. He must find some way to occupy his time, although as a rule he has to work too hard to be able to cultivate many outside interests, and the Church has no idea what to do with him. He has learnt a great deal in the course of his episcopate and it might be supposed that his former experience could fruitfully be employed by the Church, but in fact nobody seeks his advice. The Church writes him off altogether.'

This passage in itself indicates how great a change has overtaken the ministry of the Church in the years since Russell Barry wrote it. Most bishops today look forward to retirement and revel in it when it comes. Bureaucracy breeds bureaucracy. The official duties of a bishop have become even more exhausting than they were thirty years ago. The clergy are walking on the quicksands rather than in the secure citadel of a freehold. As a result, they are not nearly so possessive of their office and status as once they were and do not take themselves so seriously. Russell and his contemporaries like Williams, Haigh, and Hunter, were all busy men in their dioceses, but they had been reared in a less hurried and more gracious and spacious age than our own. They were all men of erudition and culture and they never allowed themselves to become as submerged in their work as many of their successors are today. Russell allowed himself long holidays. In some respects he sat as loose to his diocese as some of the scholarly bishops of the eighteenth century had done. He grumbled at the intrusions into his leisure time for writing. But when the time came for him to retire, he was loath to hand over an office which gave him a seat in the legislature, association with influential people, and, as he thought, a position in the Church which secured more attention for what he had to say than he would otherwise have had.

Russell seldom talked nonsense. A native intelligence refined by reading Greats at Oxford had seen to that. But it is nonsense, and was proved to be in his case, that bishops must sink into oblivion after retirement. The arrival of a retired bishop in a neighbourhood where bishops have previously been seldom seen arouses some interest and he is more likely to be overwhelmed by hospitality than socially neglected. He now has leisure to indulge friendships as he never could do when he was out and about in his diocese five or six nights a week. If he has made a name for himself through some particular interest or activity, he will be pounced upon for speaking engagements which he can always refuse if he feels so inclined. The main disadvantage of retirement is that a bishop without private means will be very hard up and a great deal of his time is likely to be taken up with housework. Russell's friend, Richard Brook, after retiring from the Diocese of St. Edmundsbury and Ipswich, put 'taking the dog for a walk and washing up' as his recreations in *Who's Who.*

Membership of the House of Lords had appealed to Russell but he was not a frequent speaker there. In any case, about the time he left his diocese retired bishops were allowed to use the Lords as a club, even though they had ceased to be members. His prediction that once he had retired no-one would want to read what he wrote was falsified by events. He wrote more books in retirement than ever before. The publishers just would not leave him alone. Lord Chesterfield in extreme old age is said to have remarked to a fellow nobleman, 'My lord, the trouble with you and me is we have both been dead for ten years but have not chosen to let it be known.' Russell lived for thirteen years after retirement but with a new book appearing every year he never gave church people the opportunity of speculating about his mortality. Even more than his books, his articles in *The Times* kept him in the mind of the general public, or at any rate that section of it which reads *The Times.*

The Editor, William Rees-Mogg, regarded the Saturday religious articles as an important feature and gave every encouragement to the sub-editor, Patrick Carnegie, to maintain a high standard. They attracted so much attention that in 1974 a selection of them, 34 in all, were re-published in book form. In a foreword, Mr. Rees-Mogg wrote:

> 'With some honourable exceptions the British press has neglected religious features in recent years. With the exception of major disputes such as the Papal Encyclical, *Humanae Vitae,* the ordinary news coverage of religion has been irregular and often trivial. On *The Times* we have tried to correct this. Religion is still an active part of the life of the majority of our readers. We have, therefore, seen the Saturday articles as a way of explaining the development of thought about religion in an age both of change and doubt and yet without over-valuing doubt or change.'

Of the 34 articles by leading Christian thinkers selected for publication in the book, entitled *Christianity Revalued,* no less than 14 came from Russell's pen. That in itself is a remarkable tribute to an octogenarian. Without doubt Mr. Carnegie regarded him as the most convincing exponent of the Christian faith that *The Times* could get hold of in the 1970s. If, as the Editor suggests, *The Times* was looking for a Christian spokesman who could speak to a generation overwhelmed by rapid change, he could not have made a better choice than F. R. Barry, who had spent sixty years in attempting to preserve the best of the past and at the same time making it intelligible to the present. Russell had deliberately dipped one foot into a rapidly moving river whilst keeping the other firmly on a rock. In one of his articles he had written:

> 'The Nicene Creed can never be expendable. It stands as a magnificent affirmation of what is implied in the Christian faith and experience. Yet it is stated in terms of a philosophy which changed cultural forms have made obsolete. We may have to find other words and other categories, less abstract, more personal and dynamic, with which to communicate to the world.'

Russell spoke straight to the condition of the questing layman who wanted to be a Christian but found it difficult to accept the faith as it had been presented to him. 'Doubting Thomas has become a proverb and in some cases a cautionary tale. It has too often been supposed that "doubts" are sinful and a sign of moral failure. But in all faith there is an element of doubt and a living faith will be a questing faith . . . There is no dichotomy between faith and reason. Both are channels of divine disclosure and although reason alone can never generate faith (which is a response to divine revelation) yet faith unsupported by rational arguments is in a dangerously exposed position.' Russell had the rare gift for a clergyman of getting right inside the thoughts of the enquiring layman and of reassuring him that his doubts were not so catastrophic as they might at first appear and, in so far as religious doubts can ever be resolved, helping him to resolve them. He also had a happy knack of putting theological affirmations in non-technical language.

In an article on suffering, after speaking of the Cross, Russell ends with these words, 'I do not say this is the answer, but it is a light which illuminates and shines unquenched in the hour of darkness and I am not only quoting a pious text. This is something I have proved to be true.' He had. Only a few weeks before, his daughter's second husband had died suddenly and unexpectedly on a parish outing.

Russell gave lectures at a teachers' training college which were appreciated. But he no longer attracted crowds by his preaching. That was because increasing deafness began to affect his diction. The Rector of St. Michael's, Cornhill, appointed him St. Antholin's lecturer to his City church, but although the substance of his addresses did not deteriorate with the passing of the years, his delivery, though audible, was hardly intelligible. The attendance was humiliatingly small.

II

On retirement, the Barry's kept their house in Borrowdale which they had used for their holidays but let at other times in the year to cover the cost of the rates. Until well on in his eighties, Russell could still walk much younger men than himself off their feet. In London he rented a flat in Tufton Street, Westminster, a stone's throw from his old church of St. John's, and conveniently close to the House of Lords and the Athenaeum. He could also worship in the Abbey with all its precious memories. His mind was as active as ever. Cramped as the flat was, it provided him with a tiny sanctum in which he would tuck himself away, pulling at his pipe, reading writing and thinking. He never abandoned the habit of saying his daily office.

Russell was not happy at the way things were turning out in Church and State. As he wrote in his autobiography, most of the things he had valued in life seemed to have perished. In his student days there had been a generally accepted metaphysic which had held the intelligent theologian and the most sceptical of philosophers in its embrace. Now, to use his own pungent phrase, 'metaphysics had become a dirty word in my own university'. The philosopher of the new school and the theist were not breathing the same atmosphere nor speaking the same language. Russell in spite of his age refused to capitulate. He was still striving to build bridges, but he found it increasingly uphill work.

Neither was he at home in the church as he found it in the years after his retirement. It seemed to be losing its nerve and surrendering outposts unnecessarily. He had once asserted he would never be happy under disestablishment. The 'small church' idea which became fashionable in the 1960s appalled him. He deplored the withdrawal of the parson from the countryside, though he had to confess it was shortage of manpower rather than doctrinnaire pastoral policy that was responsible. He was surprisingly unimpressed by the attempts to provide new services. In fact his whole attitude to prayer book revision was ambivalent. All his life he had campaigned for revision, particularly in the wording of the occasional offices, but mainly he was happy with Mattins and Evensong as they stood. It was the lectionary he regarded as obscure and he wanted to revise it. But when the new liturgies appeared he wrote them off as 'these chatty little services' and, with calculated injustice, confessed to a friend, 'they will be singing "He's a jolly good fellow" instead of the Sanctus before long.' His lack of appreciation of Series 2 and 3 may be accounted for by his increasing isolation through his deafness in any sort of service, and he was therefore not able to appreciate how well these new services suited the ethos of a parish communion. As a preacher he liked to work out his theme very carefully. At Oxford and Westminster he had expected his congregation to follow his line of argument for at least twenty minutes. He had little use for the 'few words' to which a preacher is expected to confine himself after the Gospel.

In the last years of his life conversation became so difficult, almost impossible, that Russell saw less and less of his friends. Nicholas Allenby, who understood him better than any of the others, was his most frequent visitor. He appreciated the pastoral ministrations of Bill Davidson, the Vicar of his parish in Westminster, whom he had ordained at Southwell a quarter of a century before. He was glad to see old friends but found attempted conversation with them tiring. Once when a caller was descending in the lift, Russell's voice was heard booming out from the landing above, 'It was jolly nice to see him but, oh, what a long time he stayed!'

Russell had always been domesticated and during his retirement helped Lilian with the housework and did most of the shopping. So he became a familiar figure in the streets around his home. Always fastidious about his own person, he was careless about his garb. In the Lake District, the shabbiest of jackets, baggy trousers, and a dreadful old cap which looked as if it had been purchased in his student days, were not out of place. Once when he went out similarly attired in Westminster, admittedly without the cap, he shared the distinction with J. J. Thomson, a former Master of Trinity College, Cambridge, of being mistaken for a vagrant.

In 1974 Lilian suffered a serious illness. Russell nursed her with all the tenderness of which he had shown himself capable in the trenches. For a time he was responsible for the housework as well as the shopping. Two years later he, who had been so fit and wiry all his life, suffered a physical collapse from which he made a good recovery. He was able to take short walks in the Lake District again.

His three grandchildren were a great delight to him. It gave him special pleasure when the eldest of them, named after him, won a place at Bradfield, his old school, and distinguished himself as a cross-country runner as Russell himself had done seventy years before. It was a great disappointment to Russell that in the last summer of his life he was not fit enough to go down to Bradfield to see his grandson act in the Greek play.

He went on reading and writing but after his eighty-fifth birthday it was clear that physically he was beginning to break up. Lilian now nursed him as devotedly as he had nursed her a year or two before. For the most part he took his disabilities patiently, though sometimes he complained. He worried about the future, particularly about what Lilian would do when he had gone. The death of Rosemary's second husband, a country parson after Russell's own heart, was a shattering blow. For a few weeks it seemed as if he might give way to despair, but before long his faith broke through.

David Hulme once said, rather surprisingly for an eighteenth century philosopher, that reason should be governed by the passions, not the passions by reason. If in the case of Russell it sometimes seemed that the mind had the upper hand over his emotions, this was not true of him in his latter days. For now, as they say in the Orthodox Church, his head was brought down to his heart.

In June 1976 he had a coronary, and was taken to Westminster Hospital where he was nursed by a daughter of one of his Southwell archdeacons whom he had baptized a quarter of a century before. He recovered sufficiently to be moved up to Borrowdale in August, there to enjoy quietly and contentedly his garden with its wonderful views of the mountains. By the autumn he was visibly failing and he went to the King Edward VII Hospital for Officers—very suitably, considering his First World War record. He returned home to be nursed devotedly by Lilian and slipped quietly away on 24 October 1976.

Russell could have been buried within the precincts of his Cathedral at Southwell. As a former Canon he had, if he had so wished, the privilege of burial after cremation in the Islip Chapel in Westminster Abbey. As it was he preferred his body to lie in the churchyard at Borrowdale surrounded by the hills which he knew and loved so well. There was a deep significance in this choice.

9. THE WRITER

I

Just before he left Southwell, Russell was asked by the Librarian to give copies of all his books to the Cathedral Library. His answer was typical of his sometimes rather calculated modesty. 'I am very happy that my books should gather dust on your shelves along with those of the Caroline Divines.' He knew perfectly well that he had been a successful writer and that his books had been widely acclaimed over four generations, and most of them had run into several editions. But no books are so quickly remaindered and relegated to second-hand bookshops as theological works. Only a few enjoy a come-back later on. Will the works of F. R. Barry still be read in the twenty-first century?

Whether or not his books are being read now, three years after his death, they are still eminently readable. He had what Mrs. Thrale said of Dr. Johnson, a promptitude of thought and a quickness of expression which even the *Church Times* of the Sidney Dark era, unfavourable as it was to his theology, had to acknowledge. Behind all that he wrote was an immense storehouse of reading which a retentive memory kept in his mind ready to pour forth as soon as a pen was in his hands. In this context the word 'immense' is used advisedly. It does not mean just large, as Boswell was rudely reminded by Dr. Johnson when, unwisely, he used the adjective in describing a mountain in Scotland. Russell's reading in the classics, philosophy, history, Shakespeare's tragedies, the Bible and contemporary literature was immeasurable.

Looking back over sixty years of intense literary activity, Russell considered that his style had deteriorated in old age, but those who read his later books and his articles in *The Times,* many of them unaware that the author was an octogenarian, did not notice any marked falling off. He had acquired an attitude of mind and a turn of phrase in his early twenties which underwent no radical change in the sixty years that followed. He himself wistfully referred in his old age to 'the smashing drive' of his youthful writings. It never deserted him. Of course, writing as much as he did, he could hardly avoid retracing his footsteps over paths he had already trodden. Yet so light was his touch and so apt was his use of analogy and illustration, that his writings never became stale or repetitive. Theological students of the 1970s would do well to comb the second-hand bookshops for his works and to stock their bookshelves with them in the so-called 'studies' which the Church Commissioners are providing in the modern parsonages. And when an honest, intelligent, and critical, layman asks for a book which will explain the Christian faith to him in language he can understand, the vicar would be well advised to lend him one of Barry's. For it was that sort of person that Russell had in mind when he wrote his books. A reviewer in the *Church Times* in 1931 acknowledged rather grudgingly that Canon Barry 'had a public which other writers may not reach.'

II

Russell wrote his first book of any size, *Christianity and Psychology,* in 1923 before he left Knutsford. This was a subject which had been engaging his attention ever since his eyes had been opened to the complexities of human nature by his contacts with the troops in Egypt in 1916. After handling war-scarred ordination candidates at Knutsford for three years, he came to the conclusion that psychology was to be the science of the twentieth century, as biology had been in the nineteenth. But in 1923 it took courage and initiative on the part of a young clergyman to embark on a subject which was only just beginning to attract the attention of church-men. Most of the clergy were very shy of it and concealed their embarrass-ment in a display of facetiousness. 'Trick-cyclists' was the name they gave to the psychiatrists whom they came to regard as trespassers in fields once reserved exclusively to members of their own cloth. A similar sus-picion was to be shown by many of the clergy, but never by Russell, to the social worker in the Welfare State thirty years later.

In Church circles the subject of sex was only raised in hushed tones and ambiguous terms. Bishop Walter Carey walked out of the 1930 Lambeth Conference and sent a telegram to the King when he discovered that the subject of birth control was on the agenda. Even Dean Inge who had a reputation for being adventurous in the subjects he chose to discuss in the *Evening Standard* is said to have thrown a copy of Aldous Huxley's *Brave New World* into the Adriatic, and it was Inge who once wrote off the greatest psychologist of the twentieth century as 'the unpleasant Dr. Freud'.

At the end of the First World War, however, a number of distinguished theologians of the calibre of C. H. Dodd, C. W. Valentine, and L. W. Gren-sted, and clergy with extensive pastoral experience like Leslie Wetherhead and Tom Pym, had accepted the challenge presented by psychological re-search. Pym was the first in the field in 1921 and Russell followed two years later with the book in which he warned the Church against treating the new science as churchmen had treated Darwin and Huxley sixty years before. 'The tide is advancing up the religious beaches. Theology cannot always play Canute. The past is full of warnings to us here. The notorious refusal of theology to countenance or try to come to terms with the Darwinian hypothesis must be resisted . . . psychology is an ally but a dangerous ally to the Christian theologian and it seems to me that unless we are careful we shall soon find a smile on the face of the tiger and Christian theology inside'. From that time onwards, Russell was to bring psychological insights to bear on all that he wrote in philosophy, history, and theology.

Three years later, as if to justify his tenure of the professorial chair of New Testament Studies at King's College, London, Russell produced a popular commentary on the Epistle to the Ephesians under the title of *A Philosophy from Prison*. He was well qualified to undertake this because his early morning lectures at Le Touquet and Knutsford had brought the Bible to life for the students straight from the trenches. As was to be expected, he set his sights at an intelligent lay readership, showing how St. Paul had to bend and adapt the Gospel, originally preached exclusively to a Hebrew audience, to the needs of a Gentile public. 'He [St. Paul] sets forth the faith of Christ in no merely local terms of Messiah and Parousia, but in cosmic significance and dignity as the bearer of a universal purpose. Here we see how St. Paul discards, not indeed Jewish traditions or his own essential Jewish cast of mind, but all that was merely Jewish and provisional in the actual forms of his thinking and expression'. This approach which he detected in St. Paul made an appeal to Russell, who was himself attempting to liberate Christianity from forms which he now deemed obsolete in the twentieth century. One passage in particular clearly reveals an approach to theology which was to remain with him until the end of his life. In defending St. Paul from the charge of inconsistency he wrote, 'Do not most of us find after writing anything that even while we correct the proofs we have already outgrown what is printed there?'

III

In 1931 after he had brushed up his own theology at King's College, London, and in the midst of his pastorate at St. Mary's, Oxford, Russell wrote the book *The Relevance of Christianity*, which made his name as a Christian apologist, in fact made it a household word in Church circles for a generation to come. If he had lived in the eighteenth century he would have been known in the coffee houses as 'Relevance Barry'. Fifty years on, that word 'relevance' may have become a little overworked. Archbishop Ramsey spoke rather disparagingly of 'this lust for relevance', and it is unfortunately true that the more irrelevant Christianity is made to appear, the more a certain type of person is attracted to it. Russell could never come to terms with the undoubted, if regrettable, fact that large numbers of devout people have always wanted a religion in a form which ranged from the bizarre to the exotic upon which the light of reason must at all costs not be allowed to play. Against such a treatment of the religious instinct his whole life was a protest. 'Christianity must be relevant or die: or at least survive as an exotic plant of interest only to the collectors of curios.' In fact Russell was not altogether right in this assertion. Many obscurantist religions have had an enormous political and social influence on their environment.

Russell was forty years old when the book was published. It is a spring flowering of his scholarship and his extensive general reading. It was intended for a generation of people who were critical of Christianity as it had been presented to them in the years after the war, who were cynical but not entirely disillusioned. The years since 1918 had been disappointing, but there was, as yet, no threat of a further outbreak of war. The figure of Hitler had not yet appeared above the horizon. It was taken for granted that Europe would never be so foolish as to resort to war again and the British Empire was still regarded as the main force for peace and the extension of civilization in the world. The acids of Modernity might be eroding away at the Christian faith, but Russell could still count on the generation to which he was addressing himself as being basically Christian. To that extent, *The Relevance of Christianity* is dated, but even after forty years much of it is still remarkably relevant. It describes a process which is still in progress.

The Relevance of the Church (1936) bears the same kind of relationship to *The Relevance of Christianity* as that of a bright boy who follows a brilliant elder brother at school and has to walk beneath his shadow for the rest of his time there. The first 'Relevance' made a tremendous impression and the second suffered in consequence of it. It was, perhaps, a mistake to include the word 'Relevance' in the title. Like its predecessor it is in part dated, but it is a much better book than some of the reviewers seemed to think at the time. They probably had not had time to digest the first book before they were called upon the devour the second.

Artifex in the *Manchester Guardian* accused the author of a lack of pastoral experience in the ordering of worship, a strange criticism of the padre who in a marquee in Egypt twenty years before could reduce a congregation of rude soldiery to an awed silence by the way he put accross an opening verse from Scripture. Russell retorted in the preface to the third edition that the passages on worship were inspired by his experience of preparing and conducting services at St. Mary's, Oxford, and St. John's, Smith Square. Even the *Church Times* admitted that this was 'a live book by a live man' and that the chapter on worship should be read by every parish priest. Russell had always been concerned with liturgical reform and was one of the company which produced the Grey Book in 1924, but his special interest was the revision of the lectionary. A prophet always runs a risk when he descends from the level of principle to that of practical detail, and Russell's forecast that any church which adopted *Songs of Praise* would double its congregation in a fortnight was palpably wide of the mark, and laid him open to the sort of charge that was made against the book by Artifex.

Most of the book was written on his way by sea to Australia in 1936. Those were the days when prolonged voyages to the Antipodes gave busy people plenty of time for leisure and for collecting their thoughts.

IV

At the invitation of the S.C.M., Russell wrote *What has Christianity Got to Say?* as soon as he returned from Australia. It was based on his sermons at St. John's and his addresses to the Luncheon Club. It marks the transition from the optimistic note he struck in *The Relevance of Christianity* to the sounding of the tocsin which characterizes everything that he wrote and said on the eve of the war. What a reviewer had described unfairly as Canon Barry's 'extravagant optimism' was giving way to a sombre realism. Munich was still a year ahead and the policy of appeasement had not yet been abandoned, but the whole style of the book reflects the era of balloons hanging ominously over the Thames Estuary, the digging of trenches in Hyde Park, and the issuing of gas-masks in village schools. Russell emphasized what he had already hinted at in *The Relevance of the Church* that erosion was fast giving way to demolition and that if the Church were to survive in what he called an age of iron, it must take iron into itself.

The same note is struck three years later in *Faith in Dark Ages* written, one wonders how, in the weeks between Dunkirk and the Battle of Britain. Russell is concerned with the reaction of sensitive and intelligent Christians who had prayed hard for peace and were now being caught up in a disastrous war. The title was entirely appropriate to the occasion. Candidly he admits that every national day of prayer called for by the archbishops has been followed almost at once by a disaster at sea or on land. A chaplain at 8th Army Headquarters in the Western desert had preached on the same theme in the presence of the newly arrived General Bernard Montgomery, and had been packed back to Cairo within minutes of the end of the service. A similar fate did not await a Canon of Westminster!

The war and his elevation to the See of Southwell combined with restrictions on printing material had the effect of putting Russell off book writing until the cessation of hostilities, but the war was hardly over before he was invited by the Archbishop to prepare papers on 'The Nature of Man' for the 1948 Lambeth Conference at which he was to play a leading part. This Conference was all the more important because the bishops were trying to pick up the bits and pieces after seven years of conflict. The book, when it appeared, was entitled *The Recovery of Man* and was greatly affected by what he had seen in the devastated Rhineland when he toured the British Army of Occupation in Germany in 1946.

'Disintegration of Western civilization,' he wrote, 'is exhibited most clearly and terribly by the dissolution of Hitler's Germany and it is one of the ironies of history that Germany in defeat is far more dangerous than it was in the days of her armed might.' 'The whole West', he continued, 'is handcuffed to that corpse.' Russell was right in asserting that world economy cannot prosper with a vacuum in its midst, but his prophecy was wide of the mark as far as Germany was concerned. Like many others, Russell underestimated the Teutonic power of recuperation. Nor could he have known how quickly a financial shot in the arm by the United States was to put Western Germany on its feet.

V

At the 1958 Lambeth Conference, Russell was invited to prepare papers for the debates on the Ministry and again he was prompted by his experience to produce another important book which bore the title *Vocation and Ministry*. He had now been a bishop for sixteen years and had been involved in ministry at ground level, taking careful note of its strengths as well as its weaknesses. The subject of vocation had always intrigued him. His own had come slowly and without crisis. He had no doubt reflected often upon his father's devotion as a parish priest without, as he thought, any vital spiritual experience to sustain it. At Knutsford and King's, London, Russell had been dealing directly with ordinands and at Oxford he had fostered many wavering vocations. It was, therefore, not surprising that soon after his arrival on the Bench the Archbishop of Canterbury, following the custom of making every new bishop 'do something' on a central committee, should invite Russell to be chairman of the Recruitment Committee of C.A.C.T.M. His book *Vocation and Ministry* is the fruit of a long experience.

As soon as Russell's retirement was announced, the publishers gathered around him to disprove once and for all that a retired bishop is immediately forgotten. In 1965 he was commissioned by the S.C.M. to write *Questioning Faith*. The title is characteristic, because Russell had been questioning faith for half a century. No faith, in his view, was worthy of the name if it did not contain an element of doubt. 'We need an immense amount of understanding of the reason why people are the way they are. Our job is not to scold them or preach at them but try to help them find the way in.' These words aptly sum up Russell's pastoral approach to the intelligent laity. It was always his way to educate from alongside rather than to bombard with dogma from above.

The name F. R. Barry had for the best part of this century been associated with the application of the Christian faith to actual situations and perhaps for this reason an impression had been made that he was no theologian and, for that matter, not much of a Churchman. He was accused by a reviewer of not knowing what the Church is. Who does? In fact, as passages in *Questioning Faith* reveal, he was a Church of England man to the core, both in his acceptance of its discipline and in his appreciation of its traditional worship. In taking services he hardly had any need of a prayer-book and knew all the collects by heart. He knew the Bible from end to end. Friendly as he was with non-conformists and unselfconscious in his churchmanship, he could never have been anything else but a son of the Anglican Church.

A year later, as if to prove that his mental stamina had not been impaired by the passing of the years, Russell produced in 1966 *Christian Ethics in a Secular Society* which many of his friends who remembered his pre-war writings regarded as the equivalent of *The Relevance of Christianity* brought up to date. Undeterred by the reviewer who thirty years before had criticized him for ranging far too widely, Russell surveyed the whole field of ethics: the family, sex, power politics, wealth and crime—a marathon effort for a retired bishop who had passed his seventy-fifth birthday. The Editor of *Theology* wrote:

> 'Some of the ethical problems of the world today are subjected to a real and full-blooded Christian analysis—an analysis, that is, which does not begin or end with the teaching of Jesus or restrict itself to biblical categories . . . but which draws on the Western philosophical tradition in which Christianity has incarnated and expressed itself. Past and present are subjected to the same incisive judgment treated with the same sharp abrasive.'

Russell's critique of the contemporary scene was all the more telling because on account of the massive reading of a lifetime he was able to survey the present from right inside the thinking of successive generations in the past. It was this comprehensive view that he was in a position to take which enabled him to see in their proper perspective the fashionable existentialism of the period, the charismatic movement, and the theology of crisis which were sweeping through the Church at the time.

VI

Russell was deeply read in theology and it had always been his ambition to write a really big theological book. From this he had previously been deterred by choosing to go to Knutsford rather than back to Oxford in 1919. At last in 1968 after retirement the opportunity came and he produced a book on the atonement. But as was now habitual with him, he could not put pen to paper without the intelligent layman in mind. 'On the textbook level,' Russell wrote, 'the history of doctrine can be as boring as anything imaginable and may seem to bear little relationship to religion and be really a record of abstract speculations which is how people today regard theology.' It was Russell's intention to make them think otherwise.

Throughout the book, Russell's approach to the basic Christian doctrine of reconciliation was characterized by historical and psychological insights. Theology, he pointed out, does not operate in a vacuum and, however much churchmen may be unaware of the fact, their speculations are conditioned by the age in which they live. When conservative theologians complained that modern theology of which they disapprove has taken into itself too much of the secular spirit of the age, they are merely saying that contemporary Christian thinkers are behaving and reacting to their environment as Christian thinkers have always done. There had never been in the apostolic age a defined doctrine of the atonement, and this fact in itself left the central doctrine of the Christian faith open to a variety of interpretations according to the prevailing *zeitgeist*. As an example of this Russell pointed out that Anselm's interpretation of the atonement was largely feudal in character.

VII

As if to demonstrate his versatility as a writer, Russell was next to try his hand at biography. Mervyn Haigh had been his closest friend in the Knutsford period and afterwards, when he was Chaplain at Lambeth and Russell was at King's, London. They saw each other nearly every week and went on holiday together several times on the Continent. When Russell went to Southwell, Mervyn was already Bishop of Coventry, and later, when Mervyn went to Winchester, they seemed to have drawn apart for some reason unknown. Russell may have had this on his conscience and felt that a tribute to his friend in the form of a biography was called for. On the surface the subject was an attractive one. Haigh was, in appearance, the most distinguished of all the twentieth-century bishops, with the possible exception of Lang. As a young man he had been the power behind the throne of St. Augustine in Davidson's last days at Lambeth. He was Bishop of Coventry when the Cathedral was destroyed in the blitz. When he rose to speak a hush always fell upon the Church Assembly, empty places quickly filled up, and such was the force of his personality that he could change the whole course of a debate. When Temple died he was seriously considered for Canterbury and it is quite possible that ill health which had already overtaken him was the chief reason for his being passed over. Yet there was a detachment about him which many people interpreted as coldness, and Russell with all his ingenuity did not entirely succeed in bringing him back to life. The book did not attract the attention for which the author hoped.

Russell wrote the biography of Haigh as a labour of love. It was otherwise with his own autobiography, *Period of my Life*.[1] As we have seen, he was essentially a modest and retiring man who shrank from revealing his inner self. It was the importunity of his friends which finally decided him to write his own life. But when he embarked on the project in 1970 at the age of eighty, it was without enthusiasm and the book, compared with Walter Matthews's *Memories and Meanings*, seems to have been written in a hurry. He did not bother to consult many of the sources available, including those that Oriel provided. He had never kept a diary, had not bothered overmuch about his letters, and his early papers had been destroyed in the blitz. Nevertheless, he revealed a good deal more about himself than he had ever done before, even if not enough. The fact that the book was something of a disappointment is really a tribute to Russell's existing reputation as a writer. Something superb was expected, and the book, though competent and interesting, could hardly be described in those terms.

Although Russell permits glimpses of his inner self, he still leaves his readers guessing. He played for sympathy but did not know how to accept it when it was offered. He wanted to be a bishop and yet went out of his way to put it about that he disliked being one. His finest hour had been in No Man's Land when his friends were being blown to pieces around him, but he was absurdly put out by minor inconveniences such as the vagaries of the weather. He wrote and spoke lyrically about the joys of the country parson and yet would have hated to have been one himself. He habitually interpreted world events *sub specie aeternitatis* and yet there was in him a worldly streak, particularly in regard to money. When Orpen was painting Lang he confessed that he was in difficulties because he had seen seven archbishops in Lang and could not make up his mind which one to paint. Lang was the most interesting Archbishop of Canterbury of this century, but certainly not the greatest. Russell was interesting because his too was a complex character, but it is not surprising that his complexities and inconsistencies, the subtle interplay between his ego and his super ego, are not adequately revealed in this book. He was altogether too reticent a person to make a great autobiographer.

VIII

Russell's last book, written in 1974 nearly sixty years after he first appeared in print, and three years before his death, shows no obvious falling off from his early works. Apart from the domestic chores that fell to him, he was able to enjoy what Mrs. C. H. Dodd describes as 'the atmosphere of undisturbed bookishness'. He even taught himself to type. He kept the window open on the outside world through his daily reading of the papers.

In some respects, *To Recover Confidence* is a sad book. 'I have lived to see nearly everything I care for and have spent my life trying to serve and set forward suspect and derided and threatened with destruction. I am no less perplexed than anyone else. Yet I can still, by the grace of God, believe in the truth of the faith by which I have tried to live.' It had saddened

---

[1] The title was taken, significantly, from a line in his father's favourite hymn.

him that the philosophical climate in which he had breathed so freely with others at Oxford had evaporated under the influence of the Logical Positivists, making the bridge between philosophy and theology virtually impassable. It disturbed him that Religious Education in the schools was now suspected by many of the teachers as indoctrinization and described by many of the young people as 'brainwashing'. Perhaps he came to the conclusion that, had it been put across as he had put it across in the College of Education at Reading in the last years of his life, the verdict would have been different. But his complaint that everything he had stood for had been dissolved by the acids of modernity was exaggerated. If this had been true, he would not have been appreciated as he was by the students at the College of Education, or by sixth-form boys at his old school who named a debating society after him, a compliment which touched him deeply.

Russell might be old, sad, and increasingly frail in body, but, as his articles in *The Times* show, he could still speak to a generation vastly different from that in which he had grown up. He concludes his last book with these words:

'I am myself an old man. The older a man gets the more he realizes how mysterious are human life and death. However confident he may be in his fundamental Christian beliefs, he will probably be less ready to dogmatize. In a sense old men know too much. They will be wanting to put in qualifying clauses and their sentences will sound less like hammer blows.'

In fact, Russell had been putting in qualifying clauses about the forms in which Christian dogma has been presented from the moment he first put pen to paper as a writer, and he was hammering away at old themes with unabated drive and determination to within a few months of his death.

10. CONTENT OF HIS WRITINGS

I

Russell Barry prided himself on being a humanist and therein lies any understanding of him as a theologian. 'Humanism', he wrote, 'stands for man's dignity and unique prerogative'. From his boyhood onwards he had steeped himself in the Classics, Shakespeare, and Wordsworth, and at Oriel he had given a lecture to a learned undergraduate society on Botticelli. He was a child of the Renaissance. But he was a humanist with a difference. Though never conventionally religious ('Religion' he said, 'is a dangerous draught'), he had caught a religious attitude to life from his father and, though very far from being churchy, he was a devoted son of the Church of England. He knew the Bible from end to end and he habitually turned to the Book of Common Prayer for spiritual comfort.

Russell's humanism was fed by his theology and his theology nourished by his humanism. He was convinced that no satisfactory theory of humanity could long survive without a theory about God. The titles of two of his books, *Recovery of Man* and *Recovery of Confidence,* bear out this point of view. 'You can't believe for long in man if you don't believe in something more than man . . . secular hope without Christian roots withers under the blast of disappointment and sinks into historical determinism or else into cynicism and despair.' But he was well aware that the two disciplines, humanistic and theological, had made strange bedfellows since the advance of science in the nineteenth century and even more since the philosophical revolution in the nineteen-thirties. 'The great twentieth-century myth', he wrote in *Christian Ethics in a Secular Society,* is the great twentieth-century nightmare. Man has a view of the Universe which leaves himself out, but for all he knows he is the only being capable of asking questions about it.'

Russell was concerned about the effect of linguistic analysis on credal statements:

> 'Since I first started to teach and write, the whole theological map has been redrawn and set out in a different projection. For one thing, critical philosophy has made us more alive than some of our predecessors to the limitations of human knowledge. Theology in the past may have claimed to know more than we know or ever can know. As William Temple taught us when he was growing old, we may have to begin again from what we know now. I have in my seventies and eighties had to revise quite a lot of my theological thinking.'

This confession came easier to Russell than to many other Christian thinkers of his generation, because it had been his habit to keep his theological affirmations under continuous review. His elasticity of mind never deserted him even when he had advanced well into his eighties. He was able, therefore, to take the theological explosion of the early 1960s in his stride, muttering when he read *Honest to God,* 'Can't think what all the fuss is about. I was saying as much myself forty years ago!' Some critics of Russell's writings might detect existential overtones, even a suggestion of situation ethics in them. He was certainly prepared to take risks and to embark on intellectual adventures. He could afford to do so because he had grown up with his feet planted firmly on solid ground, however rough the waters that swirled around it. 'I have managed', he wrote in his autobiography, 'to combine a fairly advanced and liberal theology with an old fashioned personal religion.'

Because Russell was himself critical of many traditional modes of making credal affirmations, he could fully understand, and indeed sympathize with, the exponents of linguistic analysis. But when some of them dismissed metaphysics as meaningless and swept value-judgments into a dustbin labelled 'NONSENSE', he clearly saw that they were undermining the foundations upon which any humanism worthy of the name was based. When he attacked them for introducing a 'glacial age' with their 'bleak and barren' insistence that no speculation was justifiable which was not open to the verfication of the laboratory, he was only saying what J. J. Thomson, a former Master of Trinity College, Cambridge, had said, 'This is like chasing a shadow in a totally dark room.' To this way of thinking, which was also his, the new school of thought had reduced the philosopher to the level of a park-keeper whose chief task it was to prevent visitors from committing a nuisance. In this case the nuisance was to speculate about everything which Russell believed gave a meaning and purpose to life. And what worried him most was that this 'bleak and barren debate' had not been contained at the level of the High Table. Echoes of it, often in a very crude form, had penetrated the sixth forms of every secondary school in his diocese.

After the Second War, especially after the influence of Vienna had moved to Oxford in the person of A. J. Ayer, no philosopher could talk philosophy without reference to linguistic analysis.[1] Russell from his Oxford days had been concerned with the use of words and was therefore prepared for all the questions which the new turn in philosophy posed for the theologian. He had always tried to persuade his readers that the words of the Creed could be bewildering if they were not subjected to continuous analysis and re-interpretation. In *Christian Ethics in a Secular Society* he confessed to his readers that modern trends in philosophy had made him more alive to the limitations of human knowledge. He could not claim to tackle linguistic analysis at the same level as Ian Ramsey and Austin Farrer, but this much may be said for his essays into the philosophical disputes of the time. Farrer and Ramsey were almost unintelligible even to a highly intelligent layman. Russell dealt with the subject in terms that could be understood. It was an amazing achievement that an octogenarian reared in the Idealistic School of pre-1914 Oxford could summon up the energy to wrestle with modern philosophy and even to learn from it.

If Russell was prone to criticize conservative forms of theological expression, he was equally prepared to reassess the liberal tradition in which he

1 After graduating at Christ Church in 1932, Ayer spent two years in Vienna where he delved deeply into the thinking of Wittgenstein and his associates in that city. He returned to Oxford in 1935 to drop his bombshell on the University with his book, *Language, Truth and Logic*, a few months after Russell had left St. Mary's.

had grown up. Here his theological processes, which in so many ways remained remarkably consistent through his life, did undergo a marked change after 1933. 'In more areas than one', he wrote, 'original sin has destroyed the Liberal Party [by which he meant the Whig interpretation of history upon which nineteenth-century liberalism was founded].' Julian Bell, a Cambridge undergraduate who was killed in the Spanish Civil War, left behind a political testament: 'Liberalism is political romanticism. It has no innate sense of human baseness and can only move between illusion and disillusion.' Russell agreed. Reflecting on what he saw in the Rhineland in 1946, he commented, 'If man is to recover from his self-inflicted wounds, it must be through a revival of the Christian faith.' What William Temple had come to acknowledge in his sixties, Russell recognized more and more in his seventies and eighties. Like William Pitt rolling up the map of Europe after the Battle of Austerlitz in 1805, Temple was forced to scrap any idea of producing the *Summa Theologica* on which he had set his heart in his younger days. Similarly Russell wrote at the end of his life, 'The world today is one of which no Christian map can be drawn. Our task in the world is not to explain it but to convert it.' 'The faith can no longer be taken for granted. It was killed in action on the Somme and cremated at Hiroshima and Auschwitz . . . the little domesticated world of Aquinas and Dante has gone for ever.' By the end of his life, Russell whose thinking had been profoundly influenced by Niebuhr, came to realize fully the importance of the doctrine of original sin not only in theological thinking but in political attitudes as well.

Russell worked hard to discover a meaning in history to replace the abandoned nineteenth-century Whig theory. H. A. L. Fisher whom he so much admired had written, 'Other wise and more learned men than I have discovered in history a plan, a rhythm, a predestined pattern. These harmonies are concealed from me.' Russell refused to give up the quest, difficult as he found it, convinced that the meaning, though beyond history, was not apart from it. The difference between him and A. J. Ayer was that Ayer regarded the quest for meaning as futile, whereas Russell regarded it not only as worthwhile but as a solemn duty laid upon those who had the welfare of humanity at heart.

Russell's basic orthodoxy, though sometimes shaken, was never destroyed by his radical approach to it. It comes out most clearly in his criticisms of Dean Inge's Christianized Platonism which he deemed to be rather less than 'full-blooded Christianity'. Christianity was not, in his view, about man's search for God, but God's search for man and he often quoted the text, 'we love him because he first loved us', which he conceded was utterly alien to the thought of Plato.

> 'The Nicene Creed is not expendable. I am not concerned with a programme of reductionism. We have had enough of that already. No one who takes religion seriously will respond to an offer of faith on the cheap. It is too precious a thing to be remaindered like a book that has ceased to command a sale.'

> 'The Creeds, the great dogmatic affirmations, remain as symbols of tested faith and experience. They give the believer a framework of

security and provide the seeker with true compass bearings and warn us against roads which end in a quagmire. Yet when it comes to spelling out the symbols, there seems to be no unchanging and finally fixed theology, not only because with the growth of knowledge it needs constant review and re-statement, but because revaluation is progressive and not yet complete. Its full content is yet to be disclosed. What is permanent is the unchanging Christ yesterday, today and tomorrow.'

As a Christian humanist, Russell insisted on the full humanity of the Christ against those who, by implication, suggested otherwise. He often used to say that the majority of his father's clerical contemporaries were Docetists; that is, that they implied in their teaching and preaching that Jesus only appeared to be a man. 'We have made him,' he wrote, 'into a theological lay-figure concealed by a cloak of unreality, not really a human being at all, and that is how the majority of Christians have thought of him throughout the ages.' But Russell had seen and read sufficient of the leading exponents of 'the Jesus of history school' in his Oxford days not to fall into the trap awaiting the unwary in the opposite direction of 'eliminating all the mysterious element in the portrait [of Jesus] and reducing him to the level of our own minds.' 'Sharp absolute antitheses', he wrote, 'are bound to fail to do justice to the complex history of ideas . . . Christian thinking will always be on a tightrope and there will always be a danger of overbalancing either on one side of the other.' *Dieu defini est Dieu fini.*

Russell's interest in academic theology which had been previously concealed from many of his readers by his primary concern with the application of Christianity to situations was brought to light by his book on the atonement. The fact that the New Testament writers had never attempted to formulate a doctrine of the atonement had left plenty of elbow-room for Christian thinkers in succeeding generations to make their own interpretation of what had been achieved by Christ's death, with results that had not always been happy. Russell skilfully describes some of the attempts that were made. Gregory of Nyssa likened the cross to a hook baited by God to catch the devil. For Origen, it was a ransom paid by God to the devil for the rescue of hostages in his grip. Anselm saw in the death of Christ an offering made in feudal terms to placate an outraged deity. All the great Christian thinkers from St. Paul onwards have been men of their age, as Russell pointed out.

The same could be said of the modern school of thought which Russell represented. Kindness, generally regarded today as the cardinal virtue, has, as a quality, never been deeply cherished by the Church, as Aldous Huxley was at pains to point out in *Grey Eminence*.[1] On the contrary, orthodox Christians have often deemed it their duty to be very unkind to people by whom they have felt themselves threatened. In Hellenistic Christianity great emphasis was laid upon the impassibility of the deity. No Greek could conceive of God suffering. So it was that St. Augustine was able to listen to the cries of a tortured slave with what would now be regarded as cold-blooded detachment. Russell came to regard the modern elevation of kind-

1 See Kenneth Clark, *Civilization* (BBC, London, 1975) p.329.

ness to the level of a cardinal virtue as a real Christian advance. Along with Geoffrey Studdert-Kennedy in the First World War, he had come to see that the doctrine of an utterly impassible and detached Godhead could not be commended as gospel to suffering humanity. 'To the ancient way of thinking', he wrote in his book on the atonement, 'the pertinent question was how could Christ be divine if he suffered. For the modern, the question is how could he be divine if he didn't.' This subtle distinction has had a profound effect upon the modern interpretation of the atonement in particular and on the popular idea about God in general. In the past Christians thought of God as judge and themselves as defendants summoned to appear before his seat. Recently the position has been reversed. It is God (or at least theories about God) who has come under the judgment of man. Russell saw the point in this, but he was far too religious and far too well versed in the authentic Christian tradition to be carried away by this new shift in theology and not to detect its hazards, even though he had played his part in bringing it into existence.

Russell felt closer to Niebuhr than to any other contemporary theologian. He certainly quotes him more frequently than any other in his books. He shared with Niebuhr an awareness of man's essential tragedy, coupled with a warm appreciation of man's cultural achievements. Both Niebuhr and Barry became increasingly convinced of the importance of an emphasis upon original sin, admittedly in modern garb, and of the damage that had been done, politically and socially, as well as theologically, by its virtual abandonment in the pulpit since the turn of the century. But when Russell's theology began to swing in the direction of a gospel of redemption, from that of a theology of explanation, he never surrendered to the enticements of Karl Barth. 'Christianity', he wrote, 'has never said, or never should have said, that there can be no good apart from itself. Christians believe in God too much for that.' Russell's long experience in peace and war, his living faith, his wide reading, his natural sympathy and compassion, his pastoral experience as a bishop and, one might add, his sense of humour and proportion, prevented him from falling out with continental theology as violently as Charles Raven did. If he disapproved of the theology of Barth, he understood only too well why Barth appealed to many young theologians in the nineteen-thirties. He himself deliberately allowed his theology to have blurred edges, a typical English approach which occasioned the jibe of Continental theologians that Anglican theology was composed to the sound of church bells.

Russell's two-fold purpose in all his writings was to advance the Christian faith and to liberate those who had been entrapped in perversions of it, evangelical fundamentalism and catholic authoritarianism. He therefore encouraged people to ask searching questions about it. He remained a radical to the end in the sense that he went to the root of everything that aroused his interest. He was a liberal in the sense that he felt free to be a radical. He was an evangelical in the sense that he recognized man's need of a gospel of redemption. He was a catholic in the sense that he drew freely on a treasury of Christian tradition which seemed to have no limits.

He had, in fact, a most hospitable mind, so much so that he was able to hold out a hand to welcome, and also to take from, a wide variety of contemporary Christian thinking. He, who shared Davidson's Erastian tendencies, revered Charles Gore who was often such a thorn in Davidson's side. For both these great men he had a deep filial affection. He agreed with Sir Edwyn Hoskyns that theology is about religion and must never be allowed to stop short with an analysis of religion, as some of the theologians at whose feet Russell sat at Oxford seemed to do. Yet he was constantly analysing religion himself. He was in tune with what were probably Michael Ramsey's most prophetic words to the Church in the twentieth century: 'We state and commend the Christian faith only in so far as we go out and put ourselves in loving sympathy inside the doubts of the doubters, the questions of the questioners and the loneliness of those who have lost their way.' But almost Russell's last words to the Church which he had been addressing for over sixty years were a warning that it was in danger of losing its nerve. Did he realize that if this were true it might be as a result of following Ramsey's advice too literally?

II

As a humanist, Russell was convinced that Christians should be deeply involved in world affairs. That is one of the reasons why he confessed so frankly that he could never be happy in any church which was not established. It explains why he was sometimes charged by the reviewers of his books with being too much influenced by contemporary secularism. Admittedly there was an Erastian streak in him.[1] He was aware how difficult it was to act out Christian principles in the midst of fallen humanity. He had wrestled with his own conscience before offering himself as an army chaplain in 1915. In the thirties he had been a not-altogether-convinced pacifist. Like many others, when war came in 1939 he found it easier to justify resistance to Hitler than it had been to the Kaiser in 1914. He pointed out that ever since the sub-apostolic age Christians had had to grapple with the thorny problem of compromise. As soon as they had come to realize painfully and gradually that this world order was to continue into an unforeseeable future, they had been forced to choose between keeping right out of the world, or living within it with all the limitations that this would impose upon putting into practice the precepts of the Sermon on the Mount in their public relationships. Russell believed that the Church had, in the main, taken the right course after the conversion of Constantine because he was convinced it was a Christian's duty to make the best of

---

1 Erastianism is the theory that even ecclesiastical matters should be subject to a measure of state control. Russell put it the other way round. The state needs the Church connection to purify and enrich its life. The most Erastian statement Russell ever made was meant partly, but not entirely, as a joke. In reference to the part played by the Judicial Committee of the Privy Council in saving radical theologians from prosecution in the Church courts, Russell said, 'The Judicial Committee ought to be commemorated by a stained glass window in Westminster Abbey.' Bishop Hensley Henson would have agreed with him: 'Erastianism and clericalism are morbid expressions of opposed types . . . on balance I find Erastianism less profoundly hostile to human self respect than its more pretentious rival [clericalism]. The state metes out better justice than the Church.'

circumstances rather than run away from them. This was a matter to which he gave a great deal of attention in his books from 1915 to 1975, but it often laid him open to the charge of being an exponent of situation ethics, a charge which he once denied in the House of Lords.

Russell believed that flexibility in Christian ethical standards was essential. There could be no absolute code of conduct. In *The Relevance of the Church* he wrote, 'The demand for an experimental as opposed to an authoritarian ethic need not be at all inconsistent with acknowledging Christ's spiritual sovereignty. There is not much doubt that as between the two concepts our Lord himself is on the side of the modern.' He was here defending the Oxford undergraduates of the 1930s against the charge that there had been a moral declension in their generation. This Russell denied with vigour. He refused to equate Christian morality with the average moral standards of a previous age. 'Mrs. Grundy has never been canonized as a saint.' For this remark he was criticized by a reviewer in the *Church Times.* He continued, 'It is noticeable that those who resist modern insights in doctrine and ethics are in the habit of assuming that God's voice is to be heard in tradition rather than in innovation.' Here he was in accord with the young Michael Ramsey who had written, 'It is not authority, but revolt against authority, that produces creation.'

Russell had retired from his diocese and therefore from every-day contact with the parishes before what is called the revolt of youth got into full swing. But much that he wrote in his later years shows that he did not condemn the permissive society out-of-hand as did many of his contemporaries. He had a natural sympathy with rebellious youth, for had he not been one himself? He regarded, as we have seen, the boy who was 'agin the Government' as a potential asset to the school, and he was often heard to say that Christ had come to be yeast rather than cement. In 1916 the innocent young chaplain who never swore and never told a dirty story in his life excused the bawdy talk and behaviour of the troops in France. What else could be expected in the conditions under which they then lived? Fifty years later he was the right person to talk to the boys at Bradfield and the students of the College of Education at Reading in spite of his four-score years.

The originality of his approach to social questions is seen in his support for the movement to emancipate women from the inferior status which had been their lot until after the end of the First World War. Far earlier than most contemporary churchmen, he realized that women's equality with men could only be extended and maintained if they were not subjected to a decade or more of child-bearing after marriage. The memory of his mother's early death had always haunted him. So, as we have seen, he was a champion of birth control at a time when the majority of the clergy were either silent on the subject or actively opposed to it.[1] For this he was severely criticized by a reviewer of one of his books in the 1930s especially

[1] Commenting on the reduction of the size of vicarage families immediately after the First World War, Aldous Huxley wrote, 'It is time that the clergy preached what they practised.' Russell preached on the subject before he had occasion to practise it.

for 'sparing us no details on the physical aspect of marriage. His frankness repels some not ignoble instincts of humanity.' This kind of criticism was no longer made of his essays into the realm of sexual ethics in the more permissive climate after the Second World War.

Russell, for a churchman, had interested himself in psychology well in advance of his time. He did not agree with Freud that human behaviour was largely conditioned by frustrated sexual urges. But he acknowledged the part played in human conduct by the 'unconscious' and was quick to recognize that modern psychological insights had a bearing on the traditional attitude of the Church towards personal culpability, sin, and all previous interpretations of the doctrine of the atonement. He forecast that this would have a profound effect upon the pastoral, evangelistic, and educational, approaches of the Church in the years that lay ahead.

In his last books, Russell had to admit that some of the measures he had previously supported and some of the causes he had championed throughout his life were bringing about results which he had not foreseen at the time and which he now openly deplored. He had supported the Wolfenden Report and the subsequent legislation which freed homosexual relationships between consenting adults from the penalties of the law. It was his intention to free the whole subject of homosexuality from obsolete Old Testament taboos which had lingered on for 3000 years. He advocated a more understanding treatment of homosexuals and questioned whether legal penalties had any effect upon their behaviour. But he himself, as a product of a Victorian public school, was never able to shake off a disgust for the whole subject. He still regarded it as a disease which demanded pity and treatment, and he would have been deeply shocked had he lived long enough to witness homosexuals claiming parity of esteem with the heterosexual. He was also distressed that the increasing refinement in methods of birth control was breeding an alarming degree of sexual irresponsibility amongst people of all ages. He condemned the widespread and ever increasing practice of pre-marital intercourse, arguing that betrothal was not the same thing as marriage, and that if restraint were not imposed before marriage it would be increasingly difficult to practice after it. He was fully alive to the fact that contemporary circumstances were imposing an almost intolerable strain on marital fidelity and as an historian he was able to put his finger on one of the causes. He pointed out that until comparatively recent times the durability of a marriage had not depended entirely on the intimate relationships of the couple concerned as it does today, but on dynastic, social, family, economic, and in the case of primitive societies, tribal considerations as well. Now most of the superstructure which had contributed to holding marriages together since the beginning of cilivization had been removed. This, Russell pointed out, was the inescapable situation with which the Church had to deal and from which there was no escape.

III

Russell could not work up any enthusiasm for party politics, which he once rather rashly described at the time of a general election as 'shadow-boxing', thereby inviting the *tu quoque* retort from a parliamentary candidate that the same might be said of denominational differences. After 1919 and until he entered the House of Lords, he voted Conservative but without enthusiasm. To his realistic way of thinking it would have seemed impracticable to continue supporting the Liberal Party which was never likely to be called upon to form a government again. In any case, just as he was more concerned with Christianizing state education than with maintaining Church Schools, so he was more interested in liberalizing the two great parties than in concentrating liberalism in a third political party. He had in fact always been more of an independent than a liberal. But if not much interested in the vote-catching propaganda of political parties, he was intensely concerned in all matters with which politicians had to deal. For a clergyman he was extremely well informed on a wide range of political and social affairs, as his speeches in the House of Lords were to show. Initially he was well disposed towards the Welfare State and encouraged the clergy to co-operate with it wherever they could, but he always had reservations about its claim to have solved all social problems and never shared Garbett's enthusiasm for it. As the years went on he came to agree more and more with Victor Demant that the first thing required of any political or social order was that it should make full allowance for the frailty of man. 'If the Welfare State were to founder,' he wrote, 'either through financial collapse or moral irresponsibility—and neither can be ruled out—then it would be all up with freedom. The mass of the people would choose any form of political regimentation rather than economic insecurity.'

Russell accepted the growing pluralism in the make-up of British society, even welcomed it. 'The Empire,' he said, 'has come home', and he hoped that this country would lead the way in showing the world how to accommodate different elements in the population harmoniously together. But he did pose the vital question how long the nation could maintain its integrity and identity unless some basic assumptions were shared by the majority of the population.

Although Russell was a member, the youngest, of the Archbishop's Commission on doctrine in the nineteen twenties, he did not play a significant part in the COPEC[1] deliberations over which William Temple presided in 1924. Perhaps this was because he was more concerned with helping people to think straight about God, the world, and humanity, than with any precise political or economic programme. It was his purpose to provoke people into asking the right questions because he was convinced that if they did that they would find for themselves the sort of answer which would enable them to give a lead in social and political thought. Here he stood fully in the tradition of Jowett rather than that of F. D. Maurice, Westcott, Gore, and Temple.

It was only natural that many Christian thinkers at the turn of the twentieth century should have thought in terms of social collectivism. There had been a sharp reaction from the *laisser-faire* economic philosophy—characteristic of the Industrial Revolution, which had been responsible for creating vast wealth for the enterprising and fortunate, and abject poverty for the less successful. The Christian socialists found the wind blowing in their

---

[1] COPEC—Conference on Politics, Economics and Citizenship, 1924.

direction but Russell was never carried away by it. He was critical of many of the sweeping generalizations on economic matters made by his contemporaries. 'Christian teachers', he wrote in *The Relevance of Christianity* 'are apt to observe that if everyone would accept Christianity our economic difficulties would solve themselves. But unless the churches show themselves capable of constructive and realistic thinking to vindicate these generalizations, they are bound to offer futile and almost meaningless programmes.' In fact Russell never spoke the language of collectivism which came so naturally to his contemporaries. He set much store by excellence. He was a typical product of Jowett's Oxford and was no egalitarian. Indeed he was something of an élitist. Russell was convinced that Church and State depended on the quality of leadership in both and he regarded it as a primary social function of the Church to provide enlightened leaders, mentally and morally equipped for the service of the community.

IV

Ever since Le Touquet, Russell had been concerned with the training of men for ordination. At the 1958 Lambeth Conference he had been invited to take a lead on the subject of vocation and ministry. As usual he collected more material than was necessary for the paper he read and, as had happened ten years before, his researches overflowed into another book, *Vocation and Ministry*.

As was to be expected he put vocation in the widest possible context, not confining it to the ordained ministry. He dissented from the view that vocation is something that happens exclusively to clergymen, a peculiar kind of emotional experience to which the laity remain strangers. The medieval church had fostered the idea that all secular work was sub-Christian, or at least inferior to the 'religious' vocation. Like so many other medieval ideas, this one lingered on after the Reformation. In the sixteenth century the clergy were expressly forbidden to follow what were called 'base trades', by which was meant all kinds of manual labour. Russell regarded this as a false dichotomy from which perhaps he was over-reacting when he told the grocers' wives in a mining parish that it was their business to make not only miners Christian, but the National Coal Board as well. 'One of the greatest needs of today,' he wrote, 'is a Christian philosophy of daily life', but he had to admit that under economic pressure many men and women might find themselves drifting or being propelled into jobs with which it was difficult to associate any kind of call. He hoped, perhaps rather over optimistically, that the Welfare State, then in its infancy, would provide greater scope for young people when choosing their careers.

After dealing with vocation as broadly as possible, Russell turned to vocation for the ordained ministry in particular. Quoting the calling of the original disciples, he pointed out that their following of Jesus was not apparently inspired by any kind of interior emotional experience. It was a response to a compelling command, 'follow me'. He had as a bishop always been wary of candidates for ordination who appeared to rely entirely on emotion and on a highly personalized inward feeling. 'Any religion can make people speak with tongues. It is the content of experience

97

more than its feeling tone that matters. We must try the spirits that they be of God. No intensity of feeling guarantees the value of experience or gives any real explanation of it.'

Starting, then, with the words of Jesus, 'You have not chosen me but I have chosen you', Russell argued that the Church had made a mistake in relying too much on the inner call for its supply of candidates for ordination. It was the duty of the Church to go out and recruit, a word of which he was not afraid. He was himself Chairman of the C.A.C.T.M. Recruitment Committee.[1] But if the Church was to get the right kind of candidate, it must be more explicit in presenting its case to the general public. This, as Russell reminded his brother bishops at Lambeth in 1958, should be a high priority in their list of diocesan activities.

Although he believed that the laity must in the future take a more prominent part in the affairs of the Church, Russell always had a high doctrine of the parish priest as a leader not only in the Church but in the local community. He resisted the suggestion that the work of the parson could be put into commission, and he regarded the drop in the number of ordination candidates as a disaster. The Church must always be enriching and purifying the life of the community and in that process the clergy must play a vital part.

In his enthronement sermon Russell had told the congregation that, whereas the approach of the Church in the past had been primarily pastoral, now it must be primarily evangelistic. Taking up this point seventeen years later he wrote, 'The day of the kind clergyman is over. A virtuous life and a cheery smile and a pat on the back are not enough if they ever were. What is needed now is a skilled expert, not a well-intentioned amateur.' But was that what he really wanted? Much else suggests the contrary. He had often spoken in praise of the cheerful chap about the quad who was nothing much else—a type that has been heavily represented in the ministry of the Church of England. He had often said and was to say again of the parochial ministry, 'It is not a regular number of man hours but a minister resident amongst the people sharing their lives that is appreciated.' Elsewhere he writes in the same book:

> 'The priest to whom the people are most grateful and whose ministry is longest remembered is often the man with no showy gifts to offer who simply loves God and loves his people. I don't believe anyone could spend a weekend with a good and experienced parish priest, watching him work and counting the help and blessings which it brings into other people's lives, and not recognize this as the most worthwhile of jobs.'

In the two decades after the publication of *Vocation and Ministry*, a generation of clergy has experimented with a new kind of professionalism which has included the departmentalizing of pastoral duties, the keeping of office hours and the transforming of the old fashioned parson's sanctum into an office complete with angle-poise lamps, filing cabinets, and all the paraphernalia of bureaucracy. Is this what he meant by the substitution of the skilled expert for the old-type amateur? Nearly everything else he wrote

[1] Central Advisory Committee for the Training of the Ministry—now renamed A.C.C.M.

about the pastoral ministry suggests a negative answer to that question. Anyone who wrote as much or as widely as he did is bound to be caught out from time to time in inconsistencies.

Russell defended the extension of C.A.C.T.M.'s authority against the charge that it had detracted from the authority of the bishops and had been responsible for turning away men who would have made good parish priests. We have seen that he had come to the conclusion that he had opened the doors too wide at Knutsford and had subsequently advocated the highest all-round standards in selection. One criticism of the selection boards he did make. For many years after their inception all the selectors had been male. Russell deplored the exclusion of women. This led him on to a prophecy which may well be proved by events to be accurate:

'A priesthood which excludes half of mankind from its membership can only claim to be representative in a very peculiar sense. The claim of women is logically unanswerable. I have little doubt that within the present century, though probably not in my lifetime, the Church will have been guided to concede it.'

This prophecy was made in the 1930s' forty years before a majority of the General Synod decided that there were no theological objections to the ordination of women to the priesthood.

Although Russell regarded the parochial clergy as the backbone of the Church of England, he was well in advance of his time in his advocacy of auxiliary ministries, recommending them before a shortage of regular clergy brought the need of them to the notice of the Church. Russell advocated this step on principle rather than on the grounds of expediency. He thought that priests with roots in the secular field would help to bridge the gulf between the cleric and the layman and admit a healthy lay breeze into the stuffy atmosphere of the sanctuary. Priests who continued in secular employment after ordination, he hoped, would retain valuable insights into industry, trade, and business. Whether his hopes and expectations have been fulfilled is a matter about which time alone will tell.

When the majority of the laity in the parishes and not a few of his brother bishops were deploring a tendency amongst parsons' wives to go out to work, Russell defended the practice, partly because he had no objection to the incomes of the parsonage being increased in this way, but also because he thought that a clergyman with a wife working in the world outside would be more likely to be kept in touch with his environment. He did not foresee that this new feature in parish life would effectively reduce the mobility of the clergy just at a time when the rationalization of official benefice incomes was about to facilitate it. A clergyman with a wife on perhaps a larger income than his own may be discouraged from moving to another sphere of activity. But Russell may be forgiven along with many others for not always foreseeing the outcome of some of the measures he advocated.

V

In a general review of the situation in which the Church found itself in the 1970s, Russell deplored what he regarded as a loss of nerve—a 'death wish, and a tendency to surrender strongholds before they were seriously threatened.' He had little sympathy for the 'small church' idea summed up in the much-vented phrase of the 1960s, 'Let the Church be the Church'— which he suspected really meant 'Let the Church be a small, exclusive, inward-looking religious society'. In condemning the kind of surrender in which he thought the Church of England was too busily engaged when it still had enormous opportunities, he quoted Virgil's comments on the Italian farmers of his day, 'How lavishly favoured they are, and how little they recognize their blessings.'

He was concerned that the liberal spirit seemed to be deserting not only the leaders but also many of the junior clergy and he attributed this to a decline in the intellectual standards required of ordinands. He thought the young clergy were unimaginative, passive, and lacking in inquisitiveness. 'The boy who is always "agin the Government" is regarded by the staff as a perfect nuisance but he may be the school's most valuable asset.' 'Today, on the whole, the young clergy are far more correct, much less prepared to think adventurously, far more prone to be shocked by the bishop who would feel much happier if they would shock him. The old are the rebels, not the young.' Archbishop Fisher does not seem to have shared this view. When asked what sort of man he wanted as a bishop, he replied, 'We don't want silly men who will rock the boat.' It is perhaps not surprising that F. R. Barry did not feel altogether at ease in the last quarter of the twentieth century, nor was he happy at the way things were going in the country at large.

Russell's churchmanship is difficult to define from his books. He refused to attach himself to any one party. In *Asking the Right Questions* he paid handsome tributes to the three heroes of his youth, Gore and Father Kelly, anglo-catholics, and Davidson, the latitudinarian. He might have added to their number Llewellyn Gwynne, the evangelical. The fact that he owed so much to characters of such varied traditions in itself demonstrated the true catholicity of his own churchmanship. If a label must be attached to him, it would be that of liberal evangelical. 'What is greatly to be desired here and now,' he wrote, 'by way of preserving poise and balance is a revival of liberal evangelicalism; but liberalism ought to be an integral element of the Anglican legacy, whether for catholics or evangelicals. It should not be regarded as a third force which will tend to become too self-conscious and defeat its purpose if organized as a party movement. Yet at all costs it must be kept alive.'

Russell was well aware of all the complexities of religious experience. In spite of his essentially rational approach to dogma, no faith could command his allegiance which had not within it an element of mystery, but the numinous element in religion must never be manipulated by priests in order to mystify the laity. He realized that Christianity makes heavy demands on its adherents, but his reading of history convinced him that the Church had often made the Christian religion hard in the wrong way, loading on the consciences of men and women unnecessary burdens, forcing them to choose between intellectual integrity and an obscurantism which it was their business to reject, adding to the complexity of life where it should have been simplifying it, and cramping the style of men rather than leading them into the glorious liberty of the children of God.

APPENDIX 1

SHOULD RUSSELL BARRY HAVE EVER BEEN A BISHOP?

When Russell's promotion to the See of Southwell was announced in the late summer of 1941, many of his friends shook their heads. They predicted that he would be too impatient to make a good bishop. But what worried them far more was the fear that the episcopal mantle would stifle the prophet underneath it, and Barry as a prophet could ill be spared. He himself posed the question in an article shortly after the untimely death of William Temple in 1944, 'Is the Church so rich in prophets that it can afford to squander the gifts of God? This lesson must be laid to heart. Some re-arrangement has become necessary.'[1] In the event the fears of the head-shakers were shown to be ill-founded on both counts. Russell was far from being a bad bishop, and he continued to prophesy throughout his tenure of the See of Southwell.

Russell himself had no doubt whatsoever that he ought to accept Winston Churchill's offer of a bishopric. It is not true that he only accepted it because he had lost home and job in the blitz. In fact for some time he had been disappointed that the offer of a diocese had not come his way. He was fifty-two years of age. Mervyn Haigh, his junior at Knutsford, had gone to Coventry: Leslie Hunter, almost an exact contemporary in age, to Sheffield. Privately he wrote to Garbett complaining that he had been passed over. On paper his suitability for episcopal office was unquestionable. He had been a brilliant army chaplain at the age of twenty-eight: an outstand-ingly successful head of a college at thirty: the most eminent vicar of St. Mary's since Newman, and now an outstanding preacher in London. Achievement in any of these spheres, let alone all of them, might have been thought to justify elevation to the episcopate.

Where else could Russell have gone if not to the Bench? Some of his friends thought a deanery would have suited him better. He confessed to his wife that he would have hated being a dean. The routine of choral services would, as in the case of Inge, have bored him stiff. He would have been out of place launching and maintaining a cathedral appeal. The restricted life of a Close would not have suited him. What about the Mastership of the Temple where he would have been spared administration, surrounded by intelligent laymen, and have had plenty of leisure to read and write? Surely this would have provided him with an ideal niche? But Russell was not interested in niches. Not only did he share with Charles Raven the mistaken eighteenth-century idea that eminence in an ecclesiastical sphere should be rewarded with a bishopric, but he also held to the view that his own particular talents should be earthed in the heart of public affairs. He believed, rightly or wrongly, that he would not be listened to with all the attention he deserved if he were not seated upon an episcopal throne, and he believed this to the end, even after he found that throne a good deal less agreeable than he had once imagined.

---

1 Russell's reflections on the lessons to be learnt from the death of Temple at the age of sixty-four are quoted extensively in Iremonger's *Life of William Temple*. It should be added, however, that Temple found it difficult to delegate, whereas Russell as a bishop had no scruples about abandoning quite a lot of his work to his staff.

In his last book Russell seems to give the answer to the question that some of his friends are still asking. Before becoming a bishop his ministry had been conspicuously successful. But it had been worked out in rarefied contexts, King's College, London, Oxford, and Westminster. As a prophet he had been telling his fellow Christians what they should think and what they should do, especially what they should think. But his monitions had been delivered from privileged platforms. After becoming a bishop he was forced to identify himself with the workaday church, its failures as well as its achievements. This may have been a traumatic experience, but it had the effect of forcing F. R. Barry to do his thinking from inside. He continued to write books all through his episcopate and afterwards and they were better books for his having had diocesan experience.

Russell was a very unconventional bishop—perhaps the most unconventional in a period which included Gorton of Coventry and Wilson of Birmingham. Temperamentally he shrank from immersing himself in diocesan administration and quite openly showed little interest in many of the affairs which exercised the minds and energies of the clergy. When he came to Southwell it was expected that he would be first and foremost a layman's bishop. Strangely enough as the years went by it was the clergy more than the laity who came to love and admire him. To the laity he was always something of an enigma. Russell's 'half smile', whimsical ways, quips, pathos, complete lack of pomposity, and concern for their welfare, won his way to the hearts of the clergy and offset the barrier caused by his deafness. The enigma of Russell's episcopate is summed up in the words of Alan Richardson who as Professor of Theology in the University of Nottingham valued him as a fellow theologian but also knew a good deal about him as the local bishop. 'It is eminently right and proper that F.R.B. should be a bishop in the Church of God generally. But rather unfortunate for the actual diocese directly involved.' A senior incumbent in the diocese said much the same thing: 'He was a great bishop. Whether he was a good one is a different matter.' But let a country vicar have the last word. 'The kindest and most pastorally caring bishop I ever knew.'

When a see becomes vacant and the Prime Minister's ecclesiastical secretary comes down to consult with representatives of the diocese about the next appointment, he is generally told by the Vacancy-in-See Committee that the diocese wants a man with long parochial experience. What they are asking for is 'someone like the vicar writ large'. This was not Russell's conception of episcopate. Although he often dropped in to see his clergy without warning in the most friendly and unassuming way, he did not conceive it his duty to be constantly running around the diocese, as he put it, 'blessing hassocks'. He did not want to be bothered with every detail of parochial activity. He was aware that he was different from the majority of the clergy and he never tried to be anything else because he believed that by being different he would stretch their minds and give them a wider horizon. In this he certainly succeeded. Unlike the successful parish priest who has been elevated to a bishopric, Russell won his way into the affections of the clergy by quite openly admitting that in many respects they were doing their job better than he could have done it himself.

As we have seen, after the departure of Garbett Russell did not establish close relationships with newcomers on the Bench. The younger bishops tended to regard him as something of an 'odd man out'. But without doubt he conferred a great intellectual distinction on the Bench of Bishops which was sorely needed at the time. He was a leading figure at the Lambeth Conference of 1948. His great contribution to the life of the Church was that he represented nineteenth-century liberal scholarship in the era of the Welfare State. He was a link between two ages, not a relic from one of them. He believed that he could make his contribution best with a seat on the Bench and was prepared to pay the price. The Diocese of Southwell also paid the price and after a preliminary turning of the change in its pocket cheerfully and gratefully agreed it was worth it. He has now become a legend. But there is still a lingering impression abroad that F. R. Barry should not have been a bishop. It is not shared by those who knew him best in the county of Nottingham.

APPENDIX 2: BOOKS BY F. R. BARRY

1914   *The War and Christian Ethics* (Blackwell)

1915   *Religion and the War* (Methuen)

1922   *One Clear Call—an Appeal to the Church of England* (Heffer)

1923   *St. Paul and Social Psychology* (O.U.P.)
      Christianity and Psychology (S.C.M.)

1926   *A Philosophy from Prison—a study of Ephesians* (S.C.M.)

1931   *Christ in University Life—Addresses* (Hodder & Stoughton)
      The Relevance of Christianity (Nisbet)

1934   *Right Marriage* (S.C.M.)

1935   *The Relevance of the Church* (Nisbet)

1937   *What has Christianity to say?* (S.C.M.)

1939   *Convictions* (Nisbet)

1940   *Faith in Dark Ages* (S.C.M.)
      I heard a Voice (sermons) (Christophers)

1945   *Christ and Leadership* (S.C.M.)

1948   *Recovery of Man* (Nisbet)

1958   *Vocation and Ministry* (Nisbet)

1960   *Asking the Right Questions—Church and Ministry* (Hodder)

1964   *Mervyn Haigh* (S.P.C.K.)

1965   *Questioning Faith* (S.C.M.)

1966   *Christian Ethics and Secular Society* (Hodder)

1968   *The Atonement* (Hodder)
      Weep not for me (Religious Education Press)

1969   *Secular and Supernatural* (S.C.M.)

1971   *Period of my Life* (Hodder)

1974   *To Recover Confidence* (S.C.M.)